GILBERT ONDERDONK

The Nurseryman of Mission Valley

Pioneer Horticulturist

Gilbert Onderdonk

GILBERT
ONDERDONK

The Nurseryman of Mission Valley

Pioneer Horticulturist

Evelyn Oppenheimer

University of North Texas Press

Library of Congress
Cataloging-in-Publication Data

Oppenheimer, Evelyn, 1907-
   Gilbert Onderdonk : the nurseryman of Mission Valley,
pioneer horticulturist / Evelyn Oppenheimer.
       p. cm.
   Includes bibliographical references and index.
   ISBN 0-929398-23-8
   1. Onderdonk, Gilbert, 1829-1920. 2. Nursery growers—
Texas—Biography. 3. Fruit-culture—Texas. 4. Plants, Ornamen-
tal—Texas.
I. Onderdonk, Gilbert, 1829-1920. II. Title.
SB63.053063 1991
635'.092—dc20
[B]   90-28231
                                                                    CIP

TABLE OF CONTENTS

PART I

PART II

PART III

ACKNOWLEDGEMENTS

It was the good fortune of this writer that through personal friendship with Mr. and Mrs. Allen Butler of Dallas the private papers and records of her great-grandfather Gilbert Onderdonk as preserved by the family were entrusted to me for the substance of this book.

Those handwritten papers, within the limits of legibility, have been faithfully adhered to and presented to add to the multi-faceted history of Texas and the world of horticulture. No changes have been made in spelling or punctuation in any of the original material.

Additional material of value came from Onderdonk's great-grandson William A. Buhler of Victoria, Texas, Sally Wheeler Butler, *Victoria Advocate*, *Cuero Record*, University of Delaware Library Special Collections, University of Texas at Austin, Eugene C. Barker Texas History Center. Very special appreciation is due editor Frances Vick, Director of the University of North Texas Press, for her vision, skill, understanding of historical values, and working rapport with the author.

PART I

GILBERT ONDERDONK FROM NEW YORK TO TEXAS

GILBERT ONDERDONK FROM NEW YORK TO TEXAS

One of the most interesting and disconcerting facts concerning the recording of history, one which every student and reader should be aware of, is what and who are in the history books and what and who are not. To qualify for getting into the histories and historical novels is a matter of personal judgment and knowledge or, unfortunately, prejudice.

As Theodore Roosevelt, Jr., noted in his Foreword to the 1937 edition of Jim Dan Hill's *The Texas Navy:* "In history there are happenings which have somehow 'missed the accident of fame.' Often these are the most dramatic."

Nowhere has such oversight been more regrettable than in the case of the pioneer botanist and horticulturist Gilbert Onderdonk of Texas, who began and developed the state's production of fruit and who contributed much to the knowledge and later work of Luther Burbank in California and all their fellow natural scientists.

Yet that was only one facet of the man who came to Texas in 1851 as a 22-year-old invalid in search of health and died in 1920 at the robust age of 91. In that interim he became a Confederate soldier, a traveler throughout Mexico for the United States Department of Agriculture, a prolific letter writer and essayist, a newspaper reporter on those travels, a man of family and property and international recognition among horticultural experts in Europe for his knowledge and experiments in South Texas. It was Gilbert Onderdonk's vision that foresaw and literally planted the foundation of the vast production of Texas fruit today.

Any student of nature must be a patient person, and from his very old Dutch ancestry dating back to the 17th century, Onderdonk had inherited that virtue. Patience is requisite when a seed is planted. One waits on the interaction of soil, sun, water. Time is ally, not enemy. So, too, with the family tree that produced Gilbert Onderdonk.

From the genealogical records of handwritten script in Dutch and English, papers carefully preserved and passed down from generation to generation and now in the possession of his great-granddaughter, Sally (Mrs. Allen) Butler of Dallas, Gilbert Onderdonk's heritage emerges from 1677 in Holland. Also in that year, a century before the Declaration of Independence was written, the name of Andries Onderdonck was on the list of communicants of the Old Dutch Church at Flatbush from 1677 to 1685. There the old records show that he married and that he bought land on or near Long Island.

In Holland the name was spelled Onderdonck and that spelling was retained after immigration to the New World of New Amsterdam. Not until a 1757 notation in the record of births, marriages and deaths was the letter "c" dropped from the last syllable of the name.

Clarkstown, Tarrytown, Tappan, and Westchester are the names noted in New York as homes of the various pre-Revolution men and women who evolved a family history to become as established in America as it had been in Holland. Notable, too, is the finely written script on their old records as evidence of a high level of education.

From that long lineage and legacy of six generations emerges the name of the boy Gilbert Onderdonk, born at Sharon, New York, on September 30, 1829. He was the third of nine children born to John and Harriet (Ward) Onderdonk. His mother died in early middle age, and his father moved to Niagara County where he engaged in the real estate business and died in 1870. Perhaps the break in their home life explains why young Gilbert's letters from 1849 to 1859 in the family records were written to his grandfather, Peter Onderdonk. However, the absence of letters to his father could mean that they were lost or not kept. It possibly can be assumed that grandparents took over the care of the younger children after the mother's death.

Gilbert was a frail child, and a tendency to tuberculosis was suspected if not actually diagnosed. But poor health did not keep him inactive. He learned to limit his activity and to measure his strength. Born with a love for the outdoors, he gravitated toward gardening before even beginning to study horticulture and botany.

As an eleven-year-old boy he began to originate new varieties of Irish potatoes, and at fifteen he won all premium prizes at the New York State Fair for his twelve new varieties of potatoes.

He went to school in Homer, New York, and graduated at the State Normal School in Albany in 1849. Knowing that his health could not stand the northern winters, he set out to find a climate that would be right for him—a place where his health would improve and he could settle and work. Evidently there was family support for him during this interim.

Texas was recommended, but first the young man tried places less distant. In 1850, he drove his horse and buggy to Washington, D.C. initially, and then to Richmond, Virginia. From there he went by canal boat to Lynchburg where he could get mountain air.

It was from college and then on that odyssey for his health that his letters begin to reveal his inner strength. Of special interest is his commentary as well as his close observation of all local conditions.

No changes have been made in spelling or punctuation from the original letters.

Albany
Friday, July 27, 1849
Dear Grandparents,
    I was just thinking that [you] might like to hear from me. I do not know why I have not written before for I have thought

of it a thousand times and have as often put it off and thought to do it another time. I have not heard from you since I left you in May. My health has not been good since that time. I have not been obliged to study very hard yet this summer but expect to soon. I have not been out to Uncle James', Nicola's or Henry's since I left them in May. I have not even been to see Peter Smith, although I once started for his house but was unwell and had to come back. I have been quite unwell for nearly two weeks, but now am improving. I am very weak.

On Saturday I went to Troy to visit Dr. Holmes and family. I was very weak when I started but only intended to remain there for an hour or so, thinking that the ride and visit would be a benefit to me. But when I reached the house, I found that Dr. Holmes and little Jimmy had both got the cholera. I rendered what little assistance was in my power until I was tired out, and at the advice of a physician thinking that I could be of no more service and considering my own health I returned to Albany on Sunday. When I left they had but little hope of James, but some for Uncle. I told Aunt to write to me the next day and let me know about them. She did not and I have not heard from them since. Dr. Sheldon of Albany told me that he saw Aunt with the doctor of Clarksville going through Albany with a coffin. I do not write to her at Troy thinking that she may be in Westerlo. So I write you, and as you have doubtless heard all about it, will you write soon and let me know whether Uncle or James, or both of them did die.

The trip to Troy hurt me somewhat. I have not entirely got over the effects. The only trouble is weakness. I have been so weak as to be able to walk but a short distance. I can now walk about half a mile at a time, but it tires me very much. I am getting better.

We have from fifteen to twenty-five cases of cholera each day. No one here thinks it is contagious.

I heard from home about two weeks ago. They were all well. Mother is out at Mary's now. Mary has a daughter but a few days old. Peter is helping James get in his crops. Ours have been done. There is but little fruit in Western New York.

Please answer this soon,
                    Your grandson,
                    G. Onderdonk

P. S. If you come to Albany you can find me at 331 State Street. I am boarding with a cousin of Mother's.

                    G. O.

The following letter expresses not only the deeply religious feeling and thinking absorbed from his Methodist family but also the way he was coping with a natural depression at the time. Despite the date there is no mention of Christmas.

Mount Hope
Fairfax County, Va.
Dec. 25, 1850

Dear Grandfather,
        I gladly improve this opportunity of writing to you and telling you of my health and change of location. You remember that when we last saw each other my health was very poor. I told you that it was a possible thing that I might go South for the benefit of my health.... I started with a horse and wagon about the middle of October and reached this place about the fifth of November. I am spending my time with an old friend of Father's. My health is much better since I have come here.
        You have probably heard of the death of my dear brother. He was dear to us both but God has taken him away from us and all his earthly friends. Although his earthly hopes have been

blasted and his body laid in the tomb yet he has gained much by the exchange. Yes, I believe that he was prepared to die. He has gone to be with his sainted mother in a world far better, brighter and happier than this sinful world of sorrow and suffering.

I believe we ought not to wish him back again, for he is happier than we can be here. God says in his word that he *will do right*. Yes, I believe that he does nothing but that which is right. And however mysterious it may seem to us I believe he has done right in this case. He knows much better than we do what is best for us. How grateful should we feel that we have so good and great and Kind Being to rule our affairs and direct our destinies. May we so live that when the hour of departure arrives we shall be prepared to join the friends who have gone before us, in the heavenly world.

I should have been glad to call upon my friends in Westerlo as I came down, but it was so late in the season that I thought best to hurry on before the weather became cold and stormy. It would have been out of my way to pass near you. But if I ever return, I expect to come by way of Albany and stop and see you and the rest of my friends. How long that will be I do not know. It will depend upon the future condition of my health. Next fall if I feel well enough I expect to go to Georgia and spend the time with some planter and teach his children and then return to the Northland to visit. Some of the planters pay several hundred dollars a year for a person to teach three or four children.

I wrote a letter home last Monday. I have sold my horse, harness and wagon. I should like to hear from you.

Give my love to all my friends. If you or anyone else should write, and I hope you will, direct your letter to me, Falls Church, Fairfax County, Virginia.

I remain as ever
Your affectionate grandson,
G. Onderdonk

He did not go to Georgia to teach planters' children. Instead, with the renewal of energy and hope that can be possible for a twenty-two year old, he went home to New York State to visit his parents and other members of the family and friends. On October 13, 1851, he began at last the adventure of going to Texas for his health and future. A week later, on October 20th, he wrote the following letter.

Cincinnati, Ohio

Dear Grandfather,
    ... I enjoyed the visit at Wilson exceedingly well. My health kept improving ... Perhaps I should have enjoyed it better still had not the painful thought stole over me that I should soon leave them—perhaps forever....
    My companion finally concluded not to go to Texas, and so I have started alone....
    I have now traveled five hundred miles of my long journey, and now am spending my time in Cincinnati in Ohio. When I shall go on is doubtful. The river is so low at present that it will cost me twice as much to go from this city to New Orleans now as it would three weeks hence. But board is so high in the city that it will cost almost as much to wait until the water is high as it would to go all the way to New Orleans. If I could board in the country among the farmers it would be best to wait for the high water. I shall decide tomorrow whether to go into the country or go down the river. I have a little more than two thousand dollars to travel yet.
    There is no cholera along the Mississippi River. A man who has just returned from California tells me that it is perfectly healthy all the way to New Orleans.

You would be surprised to see what a great city this is at present. Fifty years ago there were not eight hundred people here, and now there are a hundred and thirty thousand. It is more than twice as large as Albany. It is a more regular, neat and beautiful city than any eastern city I ever saw, and there is not a tenth part as much misery and poverty as in Albany. It stands on the banks of the Ohio River and I can count more than forty steamboats at once. I am in first rate spirits and hope to continue to improve in health as I have done in the past year.

If I go on this week I shall be in Texas in three weeks or less. I shall write you again after I have been there a few months and let you know how I get along, how I like the country, and whatever else I think will be of interest. Give my love to Grandmother and all the folks in general.

I remain
Your affectionate grandson
Gilbert Onderdonk

He did go on down the Ohio and the Mississippi Rivers. At New Orleans he boarded another ship headed westward along the Gulf Coast to Matagorda Bay and the port of Indianola, just south of what later became Port Lavaca. At Indianola young Onderdonk got a horse and rode inland some 20 miles to Green Lake where several families from Virginia and Alabama had settled and to whom he had letters of introduction.

Along the way the young New Yorker reined in his horse to watch herds of deer. One herd he estimated at six hundred.

According to Mrs. J. M. Brownson, who became a staunch friend, "Life at Green Lake was of the debonair quality. There was a piano in every home." With his own cultural background Onderdonk was a welcome addition to that frontier community.

He went to work on a ranch owned by the Rev. Stephen Cocke and began learning the essentials of raising cattle, horses and mules. He was also learning to become a new man—a Texan. Excerpts from the following letters, written to his grandfather from 1851 to 1859, reveal the change in him in this new environment.

... I am in the enjoyment of good health at last. I am situated on the San Antonio River, about twenty miles above its junction with the Guadalupe. I am about twenty-five miles from where I first stopped to attend cattle. There is a young man with me from Niagara. We are in partnership, keeping horses, raising horses and mules. We have sixty head. When we get able to buy some land we shall do it and then have something of a permanent home. It may be many years because we have yet to make the money to buy with, although land is cheap. I am pleased with this country. It is not necessary to have a foot of land in order to keep stock, for the broad prairie is large enough for all, and they can eat grass the year round so that we need not cut any hay. But if we had a piece of land of our own we could make improvements and have fruit trees....

... My health is improving at a very promising rate. Indeed, I often forget that I was sick, and when chasing deer on horseback over the prairies I find my endurance much beyond what I expected after so short a stay in this country. I have not been as well in years as at present. It is said to be more healthy here near the sea than higher up the country, unless you go as far as a hundred and fifty miles or so. This brings you among the hills. It is all prairie here along the Gulf of Mexico. I am not more than twenty miles from the Gulf and four or five from the Guadalupe River....

It costs nothing to raise cattle and mules here except the trouble of herding them. They feed upon the prairies the year around. I can buy as splendid looking cows as I ever saw for five dollars a head. The steers, when three years old, for ten and twelve dollars a head. Mules are now worth fifty dollars a head. Is not that strange when a mule or ox can be raised as easily and [for as] little expense as a chicken? ...The greatest trouble with mules and horses is that sometimes they get off a few miles into the wild country and get with the wild horses and are led off by them. But there is little trouble between the Colorado and Guadalupe Rivers, for the wild horses are mostly between here and the Gulf, about ten miles distant.

The settlers suffer much inconvenience from the scarcity of timber in this part of the state, yet I prefer to settle here. A person who comes here must have means enough to buy his stock, build his house, and keep himself for at least a year or two. He should begin with a hundred or even two hundred cattle, and then after two years, he cannot fail to sell stock enough to support a family and yield a handsome profit.

This is an easy country to live in, but a man must get a start before it is easy....

I suppose you are all frozen up in Albany County. We have had some frost here but not enough to affect the leaves on the peach trees. Fruit trees are as green now in December as in midsummer; the roses and other flowers are blossoming; we can gather as fine flowers on the prairie as I ever saw, and it is warm enough to be perfectly comfortable to have the door open with no fire. I am much pleased with the country...

...Texas climate, Texas fare, Texas employment have had very favorable effects upon my health. I find that my attachments to this country are increasing. If I should continue to enjoy good health and my pecuniary matters succeed, I shall be well satisfied to spend the remainder of my days in this state.

With summer almost perpetual, the winters no colder than I have known in New York in May, with an almost endless variety of production from the fruits of the tropics to those of the North, I do not hesitate to call Texas the Italy of America. Grapes grow wild in profusion. Sugar cane and cotton grow in perfection.

How oranges and lemons will do remains to be tested, as the country is so new that the experiment is not yet made, but they do well in Louisiana a degree further north than this. Figs and bananas grow finely. Peaches succeed well though not as well as in Western New York. There are a few young apple trees in this settlement [Green Lake] that have not come to bearing yet, but they look as thrifty as any I ever saw in New York. The coacoa nut and coffee trees will no doubt grow as in the countries of the same latitude. I do not think that wheat will succeed in this part of Texas, it being too far south. Besides, flour is as cheap as in New York. Our flour comes from St. Louis. As yet we have no railroads, canals, plank roads or even turnpike roads, but we hope to have those improvements in a few years as the country is being settled very rapidly. We submit to the inconveniences of a new country for the present but hope to have comfort common to the old states as ours grows older and more wealthy.

As to society, we have every possible variety. From the best and most valuable citizens down to the most blackhearted villains that ever disgraced humanity. In Eastern Texas the society is said to be as good as that of Louisiana; but in Western Texas there is a larger proportion of rascals. Yet there are many good men amid the great mass of moral corruption. Morality is upon the increase, and public virtue is more elevated than it has been. The villains who first settled this country have, many of them, gone to California, and very many have gone to Mexico and many have killed each other.

The class of persons now emigrating to Texas is very different from what it was ten or even five years ago. Instead of cut-throats, thieves, etc., the most of present immigrants are honest, enterprising, intelligent. Many come for health and many more to build up again the fortunes they have lost in the old states. Few men of much property come here, but it is astonishing to see how quick some men become wealthy here. Our money is all gold and silver. There is not a bank in the state. (Sept. 27, 1852)

You ask what kind of house we are building. It is twenty-four feet long and fourteen feet wide, one story high, two rooms, a framed building with frame raised. The boards and shingles we made just as the cooper's barrel staves are made. That is the only kind used here, for we have no saw mills in this part of Texas. You would call our home rough looking, but it will be as good as our neighbors have and good enough to satisfy us.

You ask what crops we raise. Little except corn, potatoes, cotton and sugar cane has been tried here. They raise oats a few miles farther up the country, and I think we could do it here. The upland rice would probably do well here but has not been introduced. I mean to send to Mississippi next year for some seed and try a small patch. Vines of every kind and all kinds of garden vegetables do well. We can have tomatoes, melons, and cucumbers from April till January.

Wild fruit is abundant. Grapes, plums, wild apricots are found everywhere. You may laugh and look incredulous when I tell you that we only have to plant cabbages once and then can have them always without ever planting again, but it is sober fact. When the cabbage head is cut off several more soon grow on the same old stalk. You can't beat that in New York.

We have only six acres in our field and only expect to raise corn, sweet potatoes, peas, as our main occupation is attending our stock. We have now ninety-three head—46 are breeding mares, 23 yearlings, 15 are sucking colts, two riding horses, two stallions, two jacks, three are two-year-old horse colts, and one work mule.

It will be two or three years before we shall be ready to sell stock. We expect about a dozen more colts this spring, which raise our number above a hundred. Of the colts now born, six are mules worth fifty dollars apiece when three years old. We expect as many more mules born this season. If so, and none die, that will make twelve, and worth six hundred dollars. As there is no expense in keeping them you can see that stock raising is quite profitable here. We send our mules to Eastern Texas and Louisiana.

Besides mules, we raise horses, which increases our stock of breeding mares and give us horses to sell. They are now worth 20 per cent more than when we first purchased 56 head. As you can see we can make money very fast unless some misfortune befalls....

I learned to throw the lasso pretty well. Today I lassoed 13 head, not one of them gentle, and Crosby and myself threw them down, tied them and trimmed their manes and tails. It may appear curious to you, but an animal can be more easily lassoed while it is running than when it is standing still.

I wish you could see the wild geese here. I have seen many thousands together and so tame as to allow us to kill all we wish.

If we get time we mean to go across the river where thousands of wild horses are in one herd, and catch some colts. The best stock we have was caught from wild horses.

Corn is now worth from $.75 to $1.00 per bushel. I never saw a country where a crop of corn can be so easily produced.

You tell me of a number of our relatives who are going to Wisconsin. Well, let them go there if they choose, but Texas is good enough for me....

... My post office is still Goliad and will probably remain so unless we get an office nearer.

I am well. In fact I am as well as I ever was in all my life. I am healthy and strong and weigh 166 pounds....

We are very comfortable now at Rancho Pajarito. Our nearest neighbor on one side is one mile and a half from us. The next house beyond is three miles, and the next after that is 5 miles farther. On the other side our nearest neighbor is about a mile and a half and within the next mile there are six families. Our settlements are all along the streams. Such a thing as settling back away from water courses is unknown in Texas, for along the streams is all the timber while the country off is all prairie.

There are always plenty of deer in sight of our house, and we can get one any time. Wild turkeys, wild hogs, ducks, geese, prairie hens are plenty. I have seen deer come within 50 steps of our house while I stand in the door. But we never kill unless we want meat.

Next year we expect to raise 125 bushels of corn, peas enough to fatten our hogs, about 500 bushels of sweet potatoes. Sweet potatoes are always worth fifty cents a bushel and often more. Cotton and sugar cane and all crops are good this year. (1854)

I should like to get, once in a while, a letter from you. I know you are old and not much accustomed to write. I believe you have never written me but once. I do not expect you to write as often as I do, for to me writing is as pleasant as eating. I think you ought to write once or twice a year when I write you every three or four months.

I suppose you know that Father expects to visit Texas this coming winter. We have a good patch of sweet potatoes so that he can eat at the roots to his hearts' content. We will give him hoe-cake and vinizion plenty.

The Indians are rather troublesome this summer and we expect considerable fighting in the fall. The other day a party of eight Indians took a herd of horses from the other side of the river, near Goliad, but they soon fell in with a party of Texans who killed five of the eight. Several parties are now out scouting.

Did I ever tell you I expected to be married during the coming fall? Well, I expect to marry in about six weeks. My intended is a Kentucky girl [Martha Jane Benham], is poor, but intelligent, pious, kind hearted, rather literary in her tastes, not handsome, but fair looking, appears well in society here, and is not at all afraid of work. I could marry wealth and beauty, but I prefer solid qualities in a wife. As to beauty, it is of no value whatever, and as to wealth what would it be worth with the encumbrance of a wife whom I could not love? No, I will marry such a one as I prefer, one whom I choose for her good qualities, and then I will work and make the money.

It has been a long time since I have written you, but you must never think I have forgotten you. The aged ancestor has a claim to grateful remembrance from his descendants. I always have felt a sense of your worth and have always not only respected but loved you. My father was your child and you love him. He is my father and a good father too, and for that I love him. Thus we have a tie between us that cannot be severed. I feel affection for all my ancestors back to their arrival in America, and then still beyond that I feel towards old Holland as I cannot feel toward any other country. Yes, tradition is reason enough.

... I suppose you have learned of the birth of your Great Grandson in Texas. He is now a little over two months old—a fine child—doing well. I gave him the name of both of his grandfathers. It is John Austin Onderdonk. So you have a descendant who is a native Texan. How the descendants of a man in America become scattered in one or two generations! Myself and wife are both well.

It always seems senseless to me to hear a man boast much of his wife so I will only say of mine after a year's trial that I am well satisfied with her and believe the satisfaction mutual. She is not an angel—I do not believe people ever are in this world, but I think that she is the most suitable person I could have got. We seem suited to each other and our affection for each other has not diminished but increased.

I have had a scraper sent from New York and with it I have dug a hole in a field for water for the stock.

I want to ask one favor. You know you are old and may die at any time, so I want your degueretype that I may see how you look, and then when you are gone I shall have it by me. It could be sent by mail at small cost. My sisters sent theirs not long ago.

Everybody here complains of hard times, money very scarce. But as it is time for selling off the beef cattle raised here it is expected that their sale will make times easier. There are about 450 head shipped to New Orleans every week, and a great many more are being driven over land to Missouri. They are worth about fourteen dollars a head. Our nearest neighbor keeps about two thousand head.

Horses range from $30.00 to $75.00 of the native stock, and mules from $40.00 to $100.00.

If you were a young man I would advise you to come to Texas. There is no new country that possesses the advantages that Texas has. Stock can get plenty to eat all year, and a man need not own a foot of land for his stock. You can see that if you take away the necessity of feeding stock or fencing pasture and also of owning land to graze it, a young man with small means can do a good business upon very small capital. We have no animal in our possession that has not paid fifty per cent upon its original cost.

... I suppose our folks have long before this told you that we have a little daughter. She was born Feb. 25, 1859. She is now four months old. We have given her the name Mary because it is one of our old family names and I like it for that reason. Our children are both well, complete pictures of health. Is not that a blessing? We had a little of the disease among cattle called "black tongue." Yet it was in very mild form and scarcely any died. I expect to raise sixty calves this year. In about eight years, if we do not meet with some general calamity such as never visited Texas since the invasion of Santa Anna, I ought to have a thousand head of cattle. New Orleans, Mexico, Cuba, and New York are our markets.... The cotton crop is as fine as I ever saw. This portion of Texas is passing a very prosperous year. (1859)

A letter of interest from Feb. 12, 1856, that Onderdonk's father wrote to his parents, brothers and sisters when he came to visit his son and daughter-in-law reports his enthusiastic impression about the country and its people. He especially noted the hospitality of the new Texans, the good climate, the abundance of food and wildlife. With paternal pride he wrote: "It gratified me exceedingly to hear him [Gilbert] so highly spoken of." Though he had come by Mississippi steamboat to New Orleans, he planned to return home by way of Galveston to New York. Insofar as we know, this was his first and last visit with his son in Texas.

In later years Gilbert Onderdonk wrote a series of short memoirs about this early period as a rancher and explorer through the Indian country to the Nueces River. He entitled them, "The Onderdonk Papers," but only a fragmentary part has been preserved. Even so, the richness of personal detail gives the material very special interest.

First he tells about his choice of Pajarito Point for ranch headquarters and home, though "to my eyes a place could never look like home unless there was a woman in it." As soon as possible, of course, he took care of that matter.

The name *Pajarito,* he explained, is Spanish for "little male bird," relating it to the story of a "thorough misanthrope" called Pajarito, an Indian shunned by every tribe in the area. The killer destroyed any man, woman or child he saw with his arrows. He lived in tree tops hidden by Spanish moss.

"Neither Caranchuas [Karankawas] nor the Lipans nor even the Comanches would claim him."

Finally a party of white settlers trailed him with a dog that led them to a certain tree and there they shot him down. Onderdonk lived for five years after that "in sight of Pajarito's tree." Evidently it became a legendary landmark at what was called Pajarito Point. The locale appealed to Onderdonk because of the undulating prairie and nearness to the river and timber. Obviously, as reported in his letters, he did well there.

However, in 1853 when land began to increase in value to a dollar an acre and he heard that it still "could be bought at fifty cents an acre near Fort Merill along the Nueces River," he determined to go and see about it.

Less than eighty miles were between the San Antonio and Nueces Rivers, but it was Lipan Indian country and there were no settlements. "It was considered imprudent for one man to travel that way alone," noted Onderdonk, but when he went to Goliad to meet the men who were going with him "they backed out." He went on by himself, and it was no little adventure.

He had a good horse, a gun, pistol, dirk knife, hatchet, forty feet of rope for tethering his horse at night, a couple of blankets, and a knapsack of food.

He wrote of the beauty he saw on the trail through that wilderness—the foliage, the antelope, deer, quail. He was just as observant of any movement that might warn of Indians around or behind him. At night by his campfire he slept fitfully when the hooting of an owl could mean an Indian signal or the snarl of "a tiger" [cougar] or the growling of lobo wolves. The young man survived all those experiences and recalled them vividly.

He returned to Pajarito Point satisfied with what he had there until he could afford to buy the 360 acres for what became his Mission Valley Nurseries in 1856.

As Onderdonk approached the turning point in his life—the turn from ranching to his career in horticulture—he wrote other essays of memoir, especially about his courtship of the girl he loved, Martha Benham.

With twenty single men and only four single girls and no widows in the region, there was the keenest competition—even the threat of duels to decide matters. Young Onderdonk realized that he must use all possible ingenuity. The action he took was simple and dramatic and proved to be most effective. Riding at full gallop to the Benham home, he told Martha that a war party was being organized at Goliad against the Lipan Indians. Before joining it he had to know what she thought he should do—go or not—go or stay and they marry.

Evidently the young lady's decision was instant. "Her every nerve and muscle at its highest tension revealing her innermost thought declared most energetically that I must stay." That settled matters, and a few weeks later they began the marriage that "for 53 years brightened our lives."

Onderdonk also wrote of the continued fighting with the Indians as more and more white settlers came in to take the land. One story he recorded was of a very wild raid by the Comanches at Victoria and then "at a little seaport Lynnville some 28 miles below on a branch of Matagorda Bay where the people there escaped by boarding the schooner *Mustang* lying at their landing.... The Indians began all kinds of self entertainment for two or three days. They took feather beds from the dwellings and tied them to the tails of wild horses and turned the horses loose. Feathers filled the air while the Indians laughed and yelled.... To allure the people to come ashore the Indians hid and seemed to have abandoned the town. Two men and their wives came ashore and then the concealed Indians sprang out with their spears and killed the men and took the women prisoners and set fire to the town and burned every house.... Neighboring settlers came and ambushed the Indians, killing the greater portion of the Comanches and recaptured Mrs.

West and her companion.... I knew Mrs. West during the last years of her long life, the widow of Homer Thrall, the Texas historian. If the reader will read Thrall's *History of Texas* he will find a wealth of early Texas life."

No more of Onderdonk's own history of that frontier remains intact and legible, except for the following report on the sport of capturing wild horses:

I believe that capturing wild horses was quite as exciting as any one of our sports in early Texas life. The first requisite is that one should become a reasonably good rider before he could expect either sport or success. The second requisite is that he should have become somewhat familiar with the lazo [lasso]. Skill in the use of the lazo can only be attained by persistent practice. The lazo consists of a rope with a loop at one end. The performer has one end of his rope securely fastened to the pommel of his saddle. He opens his loop to the extent required, generally sufficient to allow a circle of about six feet in diameter. He grasps the loop in his right hand and folds the remainder of the rope in a coil of perhaps two feet in diameter and securely held by the thumb of the same hand. When ready to use his lazo, he whirls it around and around his head—thus giving it all possible centrifugal force, till the instant of sending it at his object—when he hurled the entire rope at the object intended. The design is that the loop shall enclose the part of the animal aimed at. As soon as he sees he has made a successful throw, he begins to draw on the rope and thus tighten it on his victim. After a strong animal is lazoed, it requires no small skill and energy and prudence to safely and securely manage the case. But about all the "boys" became adept with the lazo, and if one was going to lazo a wild horse, he must be up to the occasion.

I had watched the other boys in their lazo exercises and had practiced considerably on different animals before I ventured to lazo a wild horse. One day while we were on a cattle hunt in the

Calhoun peninsula, we had stopped at a small pond to rest ourselves and eat a lunch. We had not unsaddled our horses and were lying on the ground taking our rest preparatory to resumption of our journey. We heard a rumbling of busy feet not far distant. It proved to be a remuda of wild horses coming to that pond for water and almost upon us. The animals evidently had not discovered us among the tall grass that was all around us. What an excitement! None of us had a moment for reflection or formation of any plan.

The wild horses were as much taken by surprise as ourselves. It was an intense moment. There could be no consultation. Each of us sprang to his saddle in less time than one could write it. Each was guided by his own instinct. Every man and every beast involved was at his utmost.

Fortunately for us, the herd was thirsty and had not been able to yet obtain water—and our horses had been watered half an hour previous, and were in just the right condition for a good race. There being no concert of action, each of us obeyed his own instinctive mental suggestions.

For my own part, I was close to a fine looking young colt that I at once determined to capture. The remuda had some-what regained its composure and was hurrying off considerably scattered while I found myself right among the herd—all moving at full speed but I must capture my colt. I began by working the colt and its mother to one edge of the herd. Also, I observed that the young colts were not running as the mature animals, and I soon found that the colts and their mothers were all in the rear of the main remuda. When I got my colt and its mother in the right position to favor my purpose, I worked my way between the colt and its mother, then bore off to the right—keeping the colt partly behind me while the mother kept her eyes on her companions and hurried on after the herd. In this way, it was not long till I had the colt out of sight of the herd and entirely away from its mother. As it was accustomed to follow its mother, it did not really know when it became separated from her. The colt was contented to follow the horse that I was riding and so I had him all right for following me into the camp.

But the next thing to consider was *where was the camp?* Always on our expeditions we had a rule that was valuable, viz, that if we became scattered, we would rally at some given point. On this trip, we had agreed that Lone Mott should be our rallying point. So I knew I was to go to Lone Mott. But which way must I go to reach Lone Mott? The suddenness of our arousal by the unexpected rush of the wild horses while we were resting at the little pond, the intense diversities of the entire occasion as each one of our party lost sight of every other during the wild chase when each was looking out only for himself and therefore saw nothing of each other, the wild rush after the fleeing animals during which we gave no heed to course, distance, or any other consideration except the one intense purpose of capturing our selection from the herd—all of these things combined to bring about an amount of confusion that can be more vividly imagined than accurately described.

I was in a tractless prairie containing an area of about 600 square miles. I knew every distant landmark if I could only catch a sight of any one of them. But I could see nothing to guide my course. I had my colt and he would follow my horse faithfully wherever I rode him and my colt seemed really glad that he had me. I had a watch with me. I took the time of the day and from that could make a guess at the direction that the sun should be. I could also make an estimate of the probable distance passed over in the wild chase. Then I reckoned roughly at the direction of some of the known landmarks by which I could verify my location. Then I rode off in what direction seemed the most likely course towards our rallying point at Lone Mott.

Well, I found Lone Mott as quickly as any green horn could have expected to do, and there I found each member of our party awaiting my arrival. Each one had something to show that he had been in the chase.

A major interruption in his career toward horticultural experimentation came as Texas drifted into the Civil War and the Confederacy despite the opposition of Sam Houston.

Even though Onderdonk was a native of the North and all his family were there, he was loyal to the land he had adopted when Texas joined the South. Without delay he enlisted in Company C, 4th Texas Cavalry, Green's Brigade which went to New Mexico.

According to *The Confederate Military History* ... "Near Craig and Val Verde the Confederates were masters of the field, capturing prisoners and artillery. In March 1862, the command arrived at Santa Fe and in a battle near that place, at Glorietta, there occurred great loss of life. The command retreated, fighting until they reached Texas, physically worn and their ranks depleted by the loss of 500 men, and reached San Antonio."

Recruiting at Houston, they took part in the capture of Fort Galveston. Under leadership of General William R. Scurry, Waller's Battalion, they met General Banks, U.S.A., in his invasion of Louisiana. In the last engagement Onderdonk was taken prisoner and sent to New Orleans. The commander of the prison in New Orleans offered him money sent by the Onderdonk family for his release if he would only take the oath of allegiance to the United States. He refused, and so he remained in prison for eight months until an exchange of prisoners took place.

After the war was finally ended, Gilbert Onderdonk returned home to his wife and children and the losses and changes imposed by the Reconstruction Period. Fortunately, his health had withstood the rigors of combat and prison, and his Mission Valley home and 360 acres of land in Victoria County had little damage except for the general post-war economic condition.

Onderdonk now could and did enter the creative period of his life. He had been rancher, farmer, soldier. He had long waited to do what had been in his thoughts and plans, and that was to turn 70 acres of his land into the Mission Valley Nurseries, where he would begin his experiments with fruit trees.

This is a photograph of the valentine Onderdonk sent to his wife when he was a prisoner in New Orleans.

When Onderdonk did that, pioneering in Texas took a new form. For the first time a science came to that 19th-century frontier, the science of pomology.

In 1883 he bought more land adjacent to a branch of the Texas & New Orleans Railroad. There he would begin another nursery and also build a home. As the village became settled, it was named Nursery, and Onderdonk was its postmaster. From there he could pack and ship across Texas and to other states and abroad.

In 1872 he published his first catalog and in 1879 another edition, a copy of which is now in the University of Delaware Library Special Collections. Included in Part III of this book are reproductions of the 1888 catalog from the Barker History Center at the University of Texas, and Onderdonk's sketches of fruit from his 1884 catalog loaned by Mr. William A. Buhler of Victoria, Texas.

Of major importance was the classification of peaches which Onderdonk wrote and published, and which was acclaimed by H. P. Gould, United States Department of Agriculture pomologist. He wrote: "The first system worked out on the botanical classification of the peach was made by Gilbert Onderdonk of Texas and was published by the U. S. Department of Agriculture in 1887. This Onderdonk system is the one most widely recognized."

Also quoted in the July 1986 *Texas Horticulturist* is this statement from Bluefford Hancock: "Onderdonk was particularly noted for the development of peach varieties. A few of his popular selections were the 'Galveston,' 'Texas,' 'Gilbert,' 'Early China,' and the 'Onderdonk.' He developed a number of low-chilling honey peaches that were adapted to the Texas Gulf Coast and to South Texas. Onderdonk was highly technical and very brilliant.... He was internationally known for the introduction of plum varieties such as 'African,' 'Coletta,' 'Early Red,' 'Hope,' 'Munson,' and probably the best known, 'Golden Beauty.'

"He also introduced the 'Victoria' mulberry and the 'Lincoln' apple and received a medal for his pears exhibit at the Louisiana Purchase Exhibition in 1904.

"Onderdonk and the famous plum breeder, A. L. Bruce, were the first to recognize the great value of the Texas native plums, such as the 'Chickasaw,' for cross-breeding with European and Asian types to secure greater adaptibility and disease resistance for Texas growers."

Later the irony was noted that Onderdonk was better known in France for shipments of grape plants than in America. By the turn of the century, however, national recognition of his work came when he was called to Washington, D.C., for consultation with the Department of Agriculture. Then the Hon. David Fairchild, who directed the Department of Foreign Plant Introduction, sent him on three trips to Mexico to explore the plant life there.

Onderdonk had not only learned but mastered the Spanish language during his years in South Texas and was able to make connections of value with Mexican officials on the highest cultural level. He brought back stock of peaches of the old primitive Spanish strain, in addition to other native fruits and plants. He was first to document the existence of the native pecan in Mexico according to historian Pamela Puryear of Navasota in *Texas Horticulturist.*

David Fairchild was so impressed with Onderdonk's accomplishments both on the Mexico trips and at home in Nursery, Texas, that in 1920 he wrote: "Mr. Onderdonk had a marvelous fund of horticultural information. An amateur could read his book *The Classification of the Peach*, now out of print, and see at a glance the proper nature of the peach, either South or North China or Persia; and when one sees a little seedling peach tree, he can name the range of latitude where it will have health and produce the best crop."

It is most unfortunate that the handwritten essays, lecture notes and technical reports on various horticultural subjects which Onderdonk prepared for scientific journals and meetings are no longer sufficiently legible to quote accurately. Many were written on the back of seed company order forms and American Pomological Society report forms from 1903 to 1909. One he wrote on the back of a letter from Professor E. J. Kyle of the Department of Horticulture, Texas Agricultural and Mechanical College, inviting Onderdonk to speak on the subject of "The Citrus Tri-foliata For Safety" in July, 1909, for the annual meeting of the State Horticultural Society at College Station, where he often lectured.

These papers and professional writings did not survive as well in the family records as did the much earlier letters, possibly because the quality of paper and ink was not as good.

PART II

GILBERT ONDERDONK IN MEXICO

GILBERT ONDERDONK IN MEXICO

In addition to his technical reports made to the U.S. Department of Agriculture which sent him to Mexico to explore plant life there, Onderdonk kept a private journal of his personal observations and agreed to send popular reports on his travels to the newspapers in Cuero, Texas: *The Star* and *The Record*. A collection of those newspaper clippings has been kept partially intact by the family, including some of the original handwritten copies.

Following are excerpts from those press clippings, letters and journals from 1898 to 1902 preserved by his family. This could be among the earliest travel reporting by an American in Mexico to stimulate popular interest and to inform the Texas public about their south of the border neighbor at the turn of the century. No other American had reported on travel in Mexico except William Cullen Bryant in 1872.

Onderdonk had more than a horticultural interest in Mexico. One of his five children, his son Frank, was a Methodist missionary there with a church in San Luis Potosi.

...I looked up to the foot hill on which the Bishop's Palace stands. I had read in the papers, when a boy at the time, of the bloody battle fought there between the Americans and Mexicans; I wanted to visit the spot of such interesting American memories. So we took a conveyance to the foot of the mountain. It is shaped quite like a man's nose, or more as the nose would be if cut across and severed between the eyes.

The Bishop's Palace is no palace at all, but is a military post. It stands on the less elevation portion of the hill, requiring a steep ascent of perhaps 500 or 600 feet to reach it.

We climbed up the narrow way. Here and there we encountered old dismantled cannon—grim reminders of that bloody day more than fifty years ago when the boys in blue scaled that rugged height.

From the summit we had a fine landscape view. Away below us was Monterey. Still nearer was the extensive groves of aqua cotta watered by the stream that flows near the foot of the mountain. Away in the distance the great silver mine smelters.

The Mexican National Railroad wound its way so tortuous[ly] between the mountains. A train on the track looked like a toy. Up the valley toward Saltillo we could see, as if in miniature, a little town. And still beyond it—half hidden by a mountain—the next little town. Every few minutes there is the roar of an explosion in the silver mines.

Monterey strikes me as having more Americans than any Mexican city except Mexico City itself. If I were hunting a pleasant resort to spend the summer months I believe I could not find better hotels. But Monterey is a hot place, only about 1800 feet above tide land, while if one is hunting a cool place during our Texas summer he should not stop at less than five thousand feet. Saltillo is 5200 feet elevation, a delightful place.

As we continue our journey from Monterey to Saltillo we are passing through very fine mountain scenery. It is sixty-seven miles and the traveler ascends thirty-four hundred feet in that distance. If he remains on the express train he will miss all the mountain scenery from Lampazas to Camero, beyond Saltillo. In 1898 we came up on the mixed train that runs from Laredo to Saltillo. Last year I traveled on the same train from Saltillo to Monterey, so that on both occasions I passed through the same wilderness of mountains. It is the grandest I had ever seen. Most of the mountains look like great masses of lead.

Some were so steep that no one could climb them. Some times clouds were floating half way up their rugged sides or resting in some mighty gorge or even concealing the summit altogether.

As the valley narrowed we were among the peaks. The railway track meandered between them to tortuous curves. Sometimes there was before us such a cluster of peaks that they seem to our eyes a solid wall. We would question how we should get through it.

But we pass much cultivated ground. A stream of water travels the mountainside and is diverted to the fields as required. We see a great deal of wheat when we pass here in the proper season. In the last half of May I have seen the wheat harvest in full career. They raise some barley; they gather it by hand reaping hooks as they did a thousand years ago. Corn, beans, pepper and plots of tomatoes are seen.

At Saltillo we see a great many very fine apple and peach orchards. Their apples make the finest show in August and September. There is an apricot here of small size, seedlings of an established race. Such apricot trees! They would remind you of a good-sized, spreading hack-berry tree.

I need not tell you of this mountain city of Saltillo, its 30,000 people, its parks and gardens and schools. We leave friends and go onward to our loved ones in San Luis Potosi.

The railway has still to climb the great steep which we have been ascending since leaving Monterey. The grade from Saltillo to the summit at Cameros station, twenty-four miles, is about sixty-five feet to the mile. About twelve miles from Saltillo we pass through the historic battle ground of Buena Vista, where General Taylor defeated Santa Anna with four times his own men. It is just the kind of ground for a small force to defeat a larger one. This is very rough country except for a few farms.

I could not keep from making some observations to a sensible looking Mexican fellow traveler about that battle of fifty odd years ago. He said that the Mexican general was bribed to let the Americans win the victory, and that the Americans were whipped but did not have the sense to know it. I told him that we had not found that out yet.

I believe I closed my former letter at Buena Vista, Aug. 18, 1900. Continuing beyond the old battle-ground, we still ascend the mountain on a grade of 65 feet to the mile. All traces of soil culture disappear. We wind along numerous curves, generally on a dug-way, a mountain peak towering above us on the left and a deep valley on our right, but always climbing towards the summit. We are in a bleak mountain desert.

Here and there we see a tuft of mountain grass and many low weeds and a small growth of bushes new and nameless to us. We see men gathering these low bushes and wonder what use is made of them. Then as we near Cameros station we see hundreds of bales of them, baled up like cotton, awaiting shipment. I was told that they contain a gum similar to India rubber and go to San Luis Potosi to have the gum extracted. So this desert mountain is the scene of an industry.

At Cameros station we are at 7000 feet above tide water. My daughter shivers with cold. We need winter dress even in July, and this is the warmest time of the year at Cameros. A few railroad employees, wood carriers and the rubber gatherers comprise the residents of this mountain station among the clouds.

From Cameros we descend about a thousand feet in the next thirty-two miles through another mountain wilderness to Catorce station where we breakfasted.

The real Catorce is eight miles distant, entirely out of sight on the mountain three miles back of the station. It is unlike any other city in the world. It is unseen among the clouds, and it has not a vehicle of any kind, not even a bicycle. It has a singular history. The name signifies in our language, fourteen, and how this city got the name of fourteen I will tell you.

Ages ago there was a band of robbers, fourteen men. They lived in this inaccessible mountain, had their families up there, living in excavated caverns. No trail could be discovered by which to ascend. Even if a party of pursuers should get into the mountain, it was such a natural fortress, so full of positions favorable to destruction of the pursuing party, that they paid with their lives for attempting to overcome the notable fourteen.

The original band was, from time to time, reinforced by other outlaws until it gained formidable proportions and became the terror of all peaceful settlements of an extensive region. This was during the Spanish rule before the independence of Mexico. I do not know how many expeditions were made against those mountain bandits or when they came to terms.

The traveler to Catorce engages his muleteer, burros and guide at Catorce station and must be ready to start at first sign of day. Horses are not as sure-footed as mules and the burro is safest of all on what perhaps is the most dangerous route in Mexico.

At the immediate base of the mountain is a very small town. I forget its name. The little burro here begins to climb. The road is a mere shelf cut out of the hard rock of the mountain side. You look down on your left quite perpendicularly. The road is not more than five or six feet wide. The burro keeps as close to the mountain wall as he can. Your foot hangs out over the deep below you. At intervals there are widened spots for a turn out for travelers to squeeze by going in the opposite direction.

The way is so very steep that the little burro can hardly climb upward. When you can't keep from looking down into the vast depths, over which your left foot is hanging, you question yourself whether you have actually begun a plunge into the fearful deep.

You may never before then have felt that you would hug a burro, but you will reach down with both arms and give that burro's neck one of the most energetic hugs that you ever gave to anything or anybody. Oh! How you love that burro. Your guide will stick close to you, encouraging the burro and yourself—a rough looking Indian guide but of lovely understanding.

At one point you see an old smelter in the great gorge below, its tall chimney reaching upward. But you see no way to get there.

In that city among the clouds upon the mountain, the visitor finds only one level place. It was originally just a flat rock surface, perhaps half an acre. They wanted to make a plaza of the place. As there was no soil in the city, they had earth carried from the base of the mountain five miles below by the route we described. It was carried in sacks on the backs of men. It was a giant undertaking to bring up earth enough to plant trees for what is now Catorce park.

Some of the dwellings are mere excavations from the very hard rock of the mountain. The city is against the side of the rock mountain, not far from perpendicular. Rock is the all present material. Excavations are made and the debris or rock is thrown down the steep below till they have made a shelf large enough for the house and a narrow footpath. Then the rock house is built on the shelf.

As there is no soil at Catorce you may ask where the products come from to feed the 10,000 people on this unique perch of this rugged mountain. Most of the trade goes by the same wild, dizzy, laborious route by which our notes have carried the reader.

The men are at work in the 240 odd mines behind and under the city. So the women and children and burros carry the food supplies up the same difficult way.

There is a church that is said to have cost seventy thousand dollars. There is every grade of poverty and wealth that one finds anywhere.

Perhaps it may interest the reader to know something of the cemetery. Without soil they can't dig graves. But they must dispose of their dead, and as the noxious gases from decomposition of bodies will not descent but always ascent, they selected an accessible quarter higher than the dwellings. There they made excavations in the rocky wall of the mountain. A considerable cavern receives the dead. The bodies are laid away in regular order in the excavations. Rock is then piled over them until there is enough to prevent vultures or wild animals from disturbing them. Thus, one after another, the deceased take places in what we would call a ghastly burial, but the best that the poor of Catorce can give.

People of wealth can do better there. They have an excavation large enough to place a body in it and close it up carefully with mason work. And so both rich and poor find a final resting place in a form peculiar to themselves.

The people, mostly, do not like to have strangers visit Catorce. I do not know why they are unfriendly, and more particularly to people of our race. Everybody goes armed there. I would not go there to find the highest type of what we call civilization. I will relate something a lady friend told me.

Her husband was an expert in ores and mining. He had to go there on business. We have noted there are about 240 silver mines and one gold mine and one can hear the explosions at all hours.

She took her sister with her for company while he would be absent. The two ladies got tired of staying by themselves among such strange surroundings. So they began to take short walks, but they soon found out that they attracted an amount and kind of attention most unpleasant. One head after another began to be thrust out of the dwellings to glare at them with angry grimaces and unwelcome remarks.

A tall, bony female form came toward them and shrieked in a loud, angry voice, "Oh yes, you blondes, you think you look pretty with all that rigging about you," and she went on with more choice Spanish that the ladies did not care to hear. Then two men came scowling and said, "Who are these strange people? We have no use for them here nor any of their sort." And they added more choice Spanish as the American ladies, now thoroughly frightened and awakened to danger, hurried to the protection of their lodging.

I am not going to Catorce to live. I don't think any of our Texas girls will want to go there to marry. A strange combination of wealth, poverty, grandeur, savagery, and general uniqueness called Catorce.

One would think that chutes would be constructed to carry the silver ore from the mines to the foot of the mountain. But the Mexican way prevails, and the ore all goes down on the backs of burros and men—mostly men. The Catorce ore is very rich in silver. There is employment for everybody and everybody has money if they care to work.

After we leave Catorce station going south we cross the Tropic of Cancer. It is plainly marked by a white structure of mason work. On the north side in black letters are the words "Zona Temprado." On the south are the words "Zona Torrido," the Torrid zone in a country where we look northward to see the sun for a certain period of the year.

We start downward on a road graded at a fall of 130 feet per mile. We see the maguey plant in great thickets. I don't know what Mexico would do without maguey. It makes their mescal, pulka, ropes, sacks, carpets and is used for many other purposes. It is sometimes planted in rows and also as hedges along fields.

As we pass the little town of Bocas we see a grove of olive trees. The olive could be a great interest in all central and southern Mexico, but these people are not easy to get started in anything that their forefathers did not engage in.

The hedges of organ cactus are beautiful. Like the pipes of a pipe organ they present such symmetry of form. It grows to a height of ten or twelve feet and seldom does it throw off a branch. It sends out shoots from its base and these flow upward beside the parent stem. We see no samples of this cactus until we have entered the tropics. It is too tender for the temperate zone. I carried home some in 1898 and they grew till the first freeze of our Texas winter and then they were gone.

We note the red pepper trees along the ditches. Their foliage reminds me of the common mesquite of Texas. But this pepper grows upright and tall. The pepper itself grows in long clusters like grapes. It has a sharp pungent flavor—is useless. The real black pepper of commerce could be grown here, but I see none.

Sept. 1, 1900

We are close to San Luis Potosi and my pulse quickens with every moment, for I am thinking of the loved ones I shall soon clasp in embrace—my boy of six feet four inches and a half—his head above every other at the San Luis Potosi station.

The people here call San Luis Potosi (San-loo-e Poto-see), for short, San Loo-e. It has a population estimated about 65,000 or 70,000. There are possibly 15,000 Americans, Brittons, French, and Germans, at least double or three times as many Spaniards, and the rest are all native Mexicans. The Americans, British, French and Germans run mostly together, socially. The Spaniards constitute a set to themselves. They are mostly men of trade—monied men—and monopolize ordinary mercantile business. I know two Canadian merchants.

The Americans are mostly employees of the two great railways that cross at this place. Others are in mining, smelting, engines for machine power, clerks, a few teachers.

The climate is delightful, the usual temperature from sixty to seventy. If some of our Texas people who hunt for a cool place in summer would come here instead of going north it would be to their advantage. When I came here two months ago I was able to walk with the help of my cane on one side and my daughter on the other. Now I am so improved of my paralysis that I walk a mile without stopping to rest, and leave my cane at home.

There are plenty of hotels, but of course they are not up to the American standard. The buildings are all of Spanish or perhaps oriental style of construction. Flat roofs and I do not know of a shingle roof in the city. There are very few plank floors. I do not know any wooden building. The reader will infer that all are fire proof. Yes, not a fire company in the city.

The walls of all buildings are of either rock or adobe. A few are of brick. The adobe here is not like what we know at home in Texas. It is made of soil mixed with water—molded and dried in the sun. These adobe walls are generally plastered and painted. The paints come from native mines. Blue is the fashionable color.

Floors are stone or brick. The bricks are burnt adobe and of excellent quality. In every city we have seen in Mexico the external or street view of these dwellings gives no intimation of the interior. The charm is all inside—the patio. You ask what is a patio? In the center of the dwelling is a roomy opening from ground to sky, and this is the patio. All rooms open upon it and its numerous plants. In some we see orange, lemon, roses, India rubber, banana, geraniums.

These people in latitude 22 know nothing about a fire for personal comfort. They have no northers except on the Gulf Coast.

Every house is somewhat a castle with iron bars on windows facing the street. So it must be here where there is a peon population, or the family would be plundered relentlessly.

When my son started to build Trinity Methodist church here in San Luis Potosi where he preaches in English every Sunday, he studied the most economical means of transporting the rock and lime from the mountains and the sand from the Santiago River. He found the burro the chosen vehicle.

I have often watched the burro cavalcade as they came in from the mountain quarries. Each burro had three rocks, all dressed to shape for the church walls. They delivered the rock free of all expense of quarry at $2.50 (Mexican) per hundred pieces and one a quarter cents each (American money). It looked comical to me in 1898 to see these cavalcades come in, some with lime, some with sand and other with rough dressed rock.

Sometimes the street was crowded with them as they waited each one for its turn to be unloaded. Thus came the material from which arose the beautiful structure on Independence Street called *Templo de la Trinidad*, in English Trinity church.

Thus also was transported the material for every building in this city.

I have seen a cavalcade of burros loaded with long pieces of lumber so balanced that it passed along the streets without interfering with anybody or anything. Such loads of wood and charcoal as these little burros bring from the mountains! We see them loaded with alfalfa till one can hardly see their feet as they pick their way along the street and one must look closely to see the little head at all. It takes a close look to tell what causes the great pile of alfalfa to move, so hidden is the little burden bearer.

I do not know of a cistern in the city; neither is there a permanent running stream, nor is there any system of water works. But there is a system of water supply. There is one deep well called artesian. The water is pumped to the surface and sold to the people. It tastes to me like the rainwater of our Texas cisterns. The well is at the electric light plant. Others are being bored by private enterprise.

Water is carried in casks suspended on a pole carried between two men. I have also seen an upright keg on an antique pattern of wooden wheeled wheelbarrow and occasionally a water cart with a cask of water. But the great bulk of the water is carried by men called *aquadores*. A round stick somewhat bent is passed along their backs, and at each end is hung a five gallon can of water. Some carry two cans on each side, and a few carry three or even four cans on each side.

I have watched the aquadore as he starts to go off with his burden. He stoops low enough to bring his yoke to the proper position while the cans of water rest on the ground. Then he rises slowly to his full height and gives the cans a gentle swing forward and backward for the amount of motion that suits his purpose. Then he catches the rhythm of the motion of the cans and adapts to it the movement of his feet as he starts off. This causes a certain hitch in his walk. They get so used to this peculiar step that most of them walk that way all the time—even when not carrying water. So the aquadore becomes known by his walking gait wherever he is seen.

Another class of burden bearers is the *cargadores*. For a few centavos they carry every thing conceivable that is to be transported across the city. He puts your trunk on his back at the railway station, and I have seen a sofa or a dozen chairs, even a piano carried by them.

Some of these sights are reminders of the way we imagine that the antediluvians did things. Mexico is a country full of opposites. The railways stand in such contrast with the cavalcades of burros. If the primitive Adam were to return he might claim a sample of the almost universal pattern of plow here. We may say the same of the Mexican ox yoke and cart.

We meet the man with the finest of well-made modern shoes. The next man has the same kind worn by Christ while he was bodily present among men. When one travels among the mountains he meets men with the latest improved breech-loading rifles and then men with old swords that have come down from the middle ages. Men with the finest revolvers and men with the belt of old single-barreled pistols that are remnants of some former century.

One sees the oriental style dwellings of the rich and the maguey or grass huts of the poor. Here the middle class is very small.

I was surprised at the enormous number of shoe makers here. But I see no shoe stores. The rule is to go to the shoe maker. I think that would be a good rule among our people in Texas. We would thus get better shoes.

I set out to spend a few days in the hot country back of Tampico. We traveled on the Mexican Central railway eastward toward the Mexican Gulf coast. The mountain heights we descend into Tamasopa Canyon make us all shudder. Those few who live on the sides of Rascon Mountain secure the small children by ropes to keep them from falling over the precipices.

In the forests we see the kind of cedar trees that cigar boxes are made of. The moist heat produces enormous vegetation.

We come to Cafatel station. There is only a station house and four little houses for railroad hands. The name implies a coffee farm, and we stopped here on a former visit and now again to see the growing coffee.

We put up our tent among the coffee trees. I don't know how many fine calladium and rare fern plants we had to destroy to clear the ground for our tent. It was the first week of May and the tropical sun beat down between the mountains. The tall trees that sent their branches to meet each other made a grateful shade for the tent.

The first thing I wanted to examine was the growing coffee. In this region the coffee is grown in the shade. A dense forest is selected and all the undergrowth is cleared out. All the tree branches that hang to within 15 or 20 feet of the ground are removed. Then there remains on the ground a heavy coat of leaves from 3 to 6 inches deep. Under this rich mulching of dry leaves is moist soil of mountain loam many yards deep. Coffee berries put in contact with this soil soon germinate. Little care is afterwards required, but the other growth must be kept down. The mulching of dry leaves is maintained by the constant dropping of matured leaves from the trees.

The coffee tree takes the form and the style of a quince tree, but higher. The coffee leaves, at a short distance, look like the leaves of the cape jasmine. It puts out long tender shoots from various parts of the main branches. The blooms alternate on these slender shoots, each bloom about as large as a silver dollar. One of these slender shoots, full of its white blossoms, makes a beautiful wreath for the head and we tried them on the little girls of our party, our granddaughters.

We noticed that most of the coffee trees were in full bloom the first week in May, yet a few had not come into bloom and still others had already shed their blooms and were loaded with young coffee berries as large as the end of my little fingers. Still others were just forming the young fruit. There was no succession of buds, blooms and berries on the same tree.

I concluded that as the trees were all seedlings there was the same kinds of variation in variety that we find in our own fruit products. As the coffee berries attain sufficient size and weight, the limbs bend down. After the berries reach full size they change color from green to bright red. Among the glittering green leaves it presents a picture of rare beauty.

Still later the red berries darken into brown. Then the crop is ready to be gathered. Each berry contains two grains of coffee as a rule. When a berry has only one grain this grain will be round, which is what we find in the coffee of commerce.

Many coffee grains of the former crop were on the ground under the trees and sprouting among the thick mulching of fallen leaves. First, a single long root goes down into the soil. As this root grows, it pushes the coffee grain upward. I have watched a coffee grain thus standing on the taproot, projecting as a stem above the ground for several weeks before I could see any change. Then a seam in the skin opens along the middle of the grain. Finally the skin parts off and two initial leaves appear. They look like a young cotton plant in the same stage. Later it puts up a central stem as cotton does, and then grows upward like a young cape jasmine or tea plant. The coffee tree has begun its life.

After the soul stirring experience of seeing the glory of the gorge and waterfall of *Puenta de Dios,* the Bridge of God, hidden on a mountain of forest wilderness of tropical vegetation— eighty jets of water spouting from the canyon side—we went on to the flag station of *Las Crucitas* (the Little Crosses) and the *Hacienda.*

Indian faces peeped out at us from behind the bamboo dwellings. At Hacienda the El Señor gives us the bamboo house for distinguished visitors, so kind of him.

It rained all night, but our little bamboo house was good against both wind and rain. We studied its architecture. Sixteen feet long and ten or twelve feet wide, it had a door in one side and a window. Bamboo poles were placed upright and bound with vines. The inside was plastered with adobe. The roof was bamboo and the covering was of palm leaves. Not a nail anywhere. No glass. Earth floor. A good house and we were glad to have it. Every house at the hacienda was bamboo.

This fertile valley, so wide and roomy at its upper end, narrows gradually till at Las Crucitas it terminated, and the railroad goes out of it through a narrow pass in the mountain eastward.

The mountains gradually diminish in altitude toward the Gulf Coast, and the prevailing forest tree is the palm. It lends a strange beauty to the landscape here. Whichever way we turn our eyes the palms and mountains are all we see. Tall—straight—no side branches—the great crown of leaves resting up on the top—palms singly—palms in groups—palms in crowded forests.

Not too far from the hacienda we stroll by a little lake from the waters of a mountain spring. Cattle graze on the rich carpet of grass or rest among the palm trees.

A noisy chattering in the trees before us sounds like a great flock of parrots holding a jubilee. Sure enough there they are—wild parrots.

We walk homeward to our Hacienda and see a cluster of banana trees and then a mass of gorgeous flowers—the wild Mexican morning glory that bloom all year. The blooms are about four inches in diameter.

Then there were lemon and orange trees in a wild state. In a vast undergrowth I saw leaves which looked like guava and some had ripe fruit. There were great thickets of guavas—as much as twenty-five acres in some patches of indigenous origin no doubt. I don't wonder they are cheap in the city market of southern Mexico.

As we approach our hut we are greeted by the hunting members of our party who have been out in another direction using their Winchesters to good advantage and are now dressing their deer. We are eating fine venison here at Las Crucitas.

If one starts out for a long ramble he encounters frequent running streams of clear water that come out from the mountains all around us. In the valley are patches of bamboo cane growing to the height of fifty feet and as straight as a fishing rod.

Great flocks of parrots and kindred varieties of birds are seen. One may see a few monkeys but they are very shy, and we saw none that day. About fifty years ago this region was thronged with them. But a disease like Cholera got among them and exterminated the monkey population as it was then.

Sometimes we come upon a group of the curious little animals called Long Tailed Raccoons. They are generally up in the tops of the palm trees. They are after the insect life that comes up from the trash which collects at the base of the palm leaves. As soon as they discover anyone approaching they start down the trunk of the tree, keeping on the same side on which they have seen you coming. They come one directly behind another till they get about half way to the ground and then they whip around to the opposite side of the tree, get to the ground and scamper off. One must look fast to see what they look like.

They are not more than half the size of an American Raccoon. They have two or more whitish bars about the face and as many on the long slender tail. The face and mouth are long and pointed, reminding me of the ant-eater. Naturalists describe them as inhabiting the coast of the Caribbean sea.

Wild turkeys and quail are numerous. We saw no snakes. We could claim a collection of *ticks*.

Our hunters boasted of the hunting from Las Crucitas to the Micos River. They killed another deer and hung it up in a tree to await their return after more hunting. When they returned an hour later they found the deer's head, hide and bones only remaining, and tiger tracks marked the soil.

We do not go to Tampico on account of yellow fever there. Our Señor here says that the country between here and there has very rich soil but little farming is done. Mostly there are large haciendas of cattle.

I asked why he did not plant orange, lemon and date trees, also pineapples and other fruits that would succeed there. He shrugged his shoulders in the true Mexican style and said it would be too much bother—that he knew how to manage cattle and did not care for a better business.

He said there were only two drawbacks about cattle—one was that screw worms are bad all year and the other trouble was on account of lions and tigers, particularly tigers.

The stockmen value their deer because the lions and tigers prefer that flesh to that of cattle. They would kill more cattle if it were not for the large number of deer upon these ranges. The tigers are beautiful and their skins are in demand in every market. They are not easily taken. While they go about to some extent during the day, yet night is their favorite time for prowling. Sometimes if it is cloudy weather they are seen early morning or late in the day.

It is understood that if you fire at a tiger you have got to kill him as they give fierce battle. They seem in no haste to get out of one's way—are not likely to follow a man into trouble—and yet will not run off at his approach, but will crouch low, growl and await attack. If they are left unmolested they will slowly retire to their hiding place in the mountains.

One may pass very near a tiger or lion and know nothing about it as they lie crouched in the tall grass or among the bushes. To kill a tiger one wants good steady nerves—a good sure firing Winchester and confidence in his use of the weapon.

These tigers and lions are a serious obstacle to cattle raising. Since we came to this hacienda one of the peons has killed a tiger. They have very broad bodies—short strong legs—are beautifully spotted—a saucy looking animal.

The extensive cattle pens of the place were all built of palm wood. I noticed the laborers brought in some beautiful mahogany logs perhaps a foot and half in diameter. In answer to my question the manager replied he always used mahogany for gate posts and posts for drawbars. When I told him that those logs would be worth fifty dollars each in New York he quietly replied that they would make him good posts.

He told me the mahogany timber was a scattered growth on the slopes between the mountains. The gates about the houses— the doors—home-made tables and chairs were all of mahogany. The same was in the wood pile and I noticed mahogany ties in the railroad.

I noticed that on none of the roads leading off from the station could be found any sign that a wheeled vehicle had ever been used on them. No cart, wagon, buggy, not even a wheelbarrow. The people at the hacienda hauled their water on an Indian *cayuse*—consisting of two poles which served as shafts and two cross pieces bound from one pole to the other to keep them in position and support the barrel or other cargo—while the back end of the poles rested and dragged on the ground. This was the only vehicle of any kind that we saw. Everything to be transported was either dragged on the ground, carried on the backs of burros or men, or on the cayuse.

It was a refreshing contrast to find such primeval innocence within easy view of a good railroad thoroughly modern in all its equipment. But I said before that Mexico is a land of contrasts.

This hacienda of the little crosses is a fair example of many haciendas in central and southern Mexico. There are others that have elegant residences with all the appointments that refinement would suggest. But I am going to continue to believe that whatever pretentions may be contained by the most elegant haciendas yet few will be found to surpass in the genuine good graces and good will that we enjoyed at Las Crucitas.

October 3, 1900

I start for my Texas home tomorrow. When I reach home I may write some things suggested by my visits to this interesting land and compile some thoughts not embodied in what I have [written] before.

Intelligent travelers in a foreign country can hardly fail to observe the contrasts between what he encounters there and in his own land. Among the first impressions in Mexico are those produced by distinctions of caste. After about seven months of observation through three years of time I conclude that in Mexican social life the influences of caste are decidedly more so than in the United States.

While in America it would be safe to say that we have between the highest and lowest strata in society a very large proportion of middle class who really are the bone and sinew as well as the rulers of the country and without which we could never have attained our present greatness and strength.

But in Mexico the middle class is so very small as to bear little part in shaping general conditions. The institutions of a country are the outgrowth of its civilization, and its civilization is the outgrowth of its history.

We speak in Mexico of the "ruling class" and of the *peons*. Each seems to understand its relations to the other so completely as to call for little friction.

Our attention is also drawn to the matter of dress. The old-fashioned genteel suit of the Mexican country gentleman—the *charro* costume—is now rarely seen in the cities, although quite common at the haciendas. The same styles that are worn in American cities are the ruling custom of the Mexican city gentleman.

With the females the case is widely different. The elderly ladies and those in middle life adhere to the Mexican suit—*reboza*—and the same is true of the girls of the *peon* class who dress like their mothers and grandmothers and look as the old peon women. But the girls of the ruling class dress quite as do the American girls of the same age. It is likely that they will adhere to American style into womanhood. One has a fine opportunity to study such matters on the promenade of the public plaza.

It requires very little intercourse with the people to become impressed with their quite universal politeness and general good humor. Acts of rudeness are very uncommon. It is rare indeed that a Mexican is guilty of laughing at a foreigner's blunders in trying to speak their language. I have often detected a look of sympathy when a foreigner was trying to get out an idea in Spanish and could not. I am not sure that most Americans could not learn a lesson from this Mexican trait.

I do not know of a better illustration of Mexican good nature than to say that several times I have seen a lot of children swinging and jumping their ropes in the main promenade of a plaza utterly heedless that they were obstructing the way—and yet the people of all sorts in passing would smilingly turn aside and walk around the rope jumpers. Even the policemen on duty allowed the obstruction to go on rather than to interrupt a pleasant childish pastime.

Your Mexican friend is a liberal host. He will tell you that his house and everything he has is at your disposal.

Anyone should be careful what he writes about a people if he knows no more about them that the average traveler is likely to gain during a mere flying visit. Some American tourists bring with them too little respect for the people among whom they come to seek the pleasures of travel.

I have been made ashamed of some parties of American "tourists" who either carried with them or improvised for occasion a mass of rudeness that spoke poorly indeed for "the land of the free." I do not care if I do scorch some of those head-long Americans that seem to care for nobody's pleasure but their own and are guilty of so many acts of rudeness. I could name some of their acts that cast shadows over the American name.

I am so glad that the tourists referred to did not hail from Texas. I have seen several parties from Texas and I am proud never to have seen or heard anything rude about them. They went about their business quietly and were courteous to everybody. I never knew any of them to rush their snap shots upon the surroundings. Nor did they slip into possession of and carry away as souvenirs little objects of value as was done by one American party when they raided the Bishop's Palace at San Luis Potosi.

If any of our readers want to travel in Mexico they would do well to go to San Antonio, Texas and buy a ticket to any Mexican point and return. Their ticket may be for ninety days and carries stop-over privileges. Then you can do everything you want to and take your time. But never go with a *hoorah* short time, cheap John excursion.

I have many enquiries about opportunities in Mexico for Americans. So I concluded to write a chapter on this subject. That which would be a good opportunity for one person might not be good at all for another. We have seen this truth illustrated in business lines all around us. I have seen men in a military prison in New Orleans during the war between the states sit quietly and starve to death because they could not see how to make a living under the disadvantages of prison life when corrupt officials had stolen the food supplies and given them spoiled and condemned rations that would not sustain healthful human life. Then I saw others who could and did not only make a living but actually get ahead in money matters under the same restraints.

In Mexico I have seen men who went there without enough money to pay two months board or to bring them back to the United States, and yet they are now in prosperous financial condition with a good business. I know of others who went there with a reasonable amount of funds who now are men of enormous wealth. I know others there with their families who are getting what we call liberal salaries and just live well and save nothing. I have seen many stranded Americans in Mexico who are not able to make a living, with their habits, nor able to get back to the States. I do not know what is to become of them. You can hardly find a prosperous American there who has not divided his earnings with his stranded countrymen, who have become confirmed tramps.

If you can go to Mexico under some definite engagement upon well understood terms with a reliable party, that is all right. But if you have no assurances from a responsible source, then you had better be careful how you go to Mexico to hunt a job.

Keep away from saloons if you want a good job. If you do not get one by the time you have spent your reserve sum—then don't lose another day—but board the first train for a home journey.

Our people cannot go there and compete with the cheap labor of the peons under Mexican conditions. Persons who have never farmed in a climate where there is never a freeze can hardly imagine the constant battle with the noxious vegetation.

When I got to supper last night there was a generous portion of watermelon on each plate. I thought I recognized the flavor and sure enough it was a Victoria County melon, almost certainly from Nursery.

I had no idea of writing from this quaint little mountain town of Garcia, but I had some work to do here in the line of my present mission in Mexico and so I stepped off from the train. I have completed my field investigation and now have some few hours of time left me.

This is a little oasis, a little Eden in the bold, bare rugged country around it. Here there is river water and its creative influence. We see stately pecan trees and lemon trees and the Aquacata trees and their fruit, one of the most quiet retreats that we ever found. Garcia is thoroughly Mexican.

Nobody is in a hurry. Tomorrow is the time to do everything. There is one man here that speaks very imperfect English out of a population of 4,500 people. No one here has any but Indian blood. I wish I could remain longer.

The more I go about the Federal District [Mexico City] the more do I become impressed with the mass of human life that is congregated in this city. The more I go about in it the greater it seems. Then when I go out to the suburbs, nominally several miles out, and find from five to fifteen thousand in each, and really cannot see where the city ceases and the suburb town begins, I get a more impressive view of this aggregation of human life. Then when I go from one suburb to another, I cannot see when I leave one or enter the other, so continuous is the settlement, and I get an exhaustive view of this vast congestion of human occupation called Mexico D.F.

The authorities here reckon the population at eight hundred thousand and I do not doubt the official figures.

One thing cannot fail to enter the mind—that this congestion and the entire district has already reached a point beyond the means of full supply of all proper requirements for advantageous living. The supply of food is not equal to demand. Therefore prices are higher than they otherwise would be. We must remember that everything is expected to cost more at a national capital. It is surprising to observe to what extent improvements are going on. New public works, business structures and factories, and elegant private residences all attest to a growing nation and capital.

This time I write from Maltrata. The name means bad treaty. As soon as we left Mexico D.F. on July 31st we were in beautiful country, every acre covered with green. One cannot get any place here that is not mountainous. There are vast plats of alfalfa in all stages of growth from bare stubble to full height. It seems to be the chief forage plant. The corn fields are interesting to one from Texas. Some corn fields are just planted, others are ready to gather, and we see all ages and sizes of corn between the two extremes. Then the vast areas of maguey plants are a study. Many maguey farms have barley, from the freshly sown to that ready for harvest, and that already in neat stacks that adorn the premises.

Some distance out from Mexico City we came in sight of two noted pyramids, pre-historic. I shall not presume to guess their dimensions and height. For what purpose they were built and by whom are among the unwritten secrets of a lost history.

To the right of this valley we see the summits of both Popocatépetl and Estbaxitual, two mighty volcanoes with their covering of everlasting snow. To the left we see the form, away in the dreamy distance, of Orizaba holding her lofty head among the clouds and also robed in the same kind of white mantle which in her own silent grandeur she has worn through all the ages.

I am told by persons living here that during the dry season this beautiful valley is an arid waste. After we pass the station of *Esperanza* (hope) we enter wild and rugged scenery of mountains and canyons as high and deep as any we have ever seen.

At one short halt several Indian girls appeared and offered fruits to the train passengers. More Indian girls were at Maltrato station in the valley with more fruit. In this secluded little world I had a mission to perform. Since then I have been visiting other little out-of-the-way places hidden among the mountains in the line of my investigations.

In one park my eye rested upon a monster tree more than twelve feet in diameter. I was told that this was the pepper tree under which Cortez the conqueror sat down and wept after a severe battle in which he had lost many men. My mind flew back to those bloody scenes of the early sixteenth century when an ancient nation was ravaged by the invading army of Spain.

In those quaint old little towns among the mountains where I have visited the past two weeks, no vehicle of any kind moved through the silent crooked, narrow streets. Every burden was carried on the back of man or burro. Women walked with little children's heads poking out of the maguey sacks that held them softly as the mother plodded along. I have never heard one crying.

The simple style of Indian dwelling prevailed in every structure except the old church of Spanish architecture. Everything was Indian to the core. None could speak English, some could not speak Spanish, only the Indian language that had come down to them from their ancestry. These people seem to be living and doing everything as they did two or three hundred years ago.

One woman offered to sell us peaches. I wanted to see the tree. She had just enough Spanish in her vocabulary to quote price; she could not talk in Spanish, only Indian. I got a man that spoke Spanish and could understand her Indian to help me. She would not consent for me to see the tree nor could I have a cutting from it, though I offered to pay her. She believed that

51

if she allowed me to have anything to do with her tree it would surely die.

At another mountain town there was a Protestant church. These people were all kindness and showed me every orchard and garden. I got cuttings of everything I desired.

I might go into details concerning these primitive people till I should tire of writing and the reader should tire of reading and yet the subject would be only just begun.

Gilbert Onderdonk died peacefully in his sleep in his home at Nursery, Texas, on that land which he had selected and so creatively cultivated to its highest fertility. With him there in the old home were his son Gilbert, Jr. and his wife and their three daughters—Estelle, Alice and Margaret.

Lovingly they laid him to rest on that day in 1920 beside his wife, Martha, in the old Evergreen Cemetery [now Old City Cemetery] near the Guadalupe River at Victoria. The ground-level grave marker and Texas Historical emblem are as unpretentious as the seedlings he nurtured and brought to fruition for all the future.

At Nursery, ten miles northwest on the highway to Cuero and San Antonio, a very elderly neighbor of the Onderdonk family, Odis Henry, told of his childhood memory of Gilbert Onderdonk in old age, giving buckets and baskets full of oranges from his trees to all the village children.

Looking out over the now empty acres, Mr. Henry said, "He was a man to remember."

Fortunately the pioneer fruit grower of Texas was never to know that his son, Gilbert Onderdonk, Jr., would prove incapable of handling his inheritance and would lose all the valuable orchards and gardens. Today nothing remains to be seen where once a man of vision and expertise realized a dream of fertility and where the Gulf breeze of coastal southwest Texas rustled the leaves of the fruit trees and vineyards he planted and developed into such bounty and beauty. Empty fields now, but the record of his work is on the pages of the history of American horticulture and pomology.

Gilbert Onderdonk was not only a lover of the earth and its richness, but as a sincerely religious man, he saw it all as a gift from its Creator. In an oration delivered on May 23, 1892, entitled, "Is Life Worth Living," he wrote: "Can the span from cradle to the grave be made so valuable as to recompense man for the inevitable disappointments of an earthly existence?"

His conclusion and affirmation was, "A life of true devotion and service to God is well worth living."

PART III

GILBERT ONDERDONK
THE NURSERY BUSINESSMAN

GILBERT ONDERDONK
THE NURSERY BUSINESSMAN

Reprinted here is the original 1888 *Descriptive Catalogue of the Mission Valley Nurseries,* supplemented with engravings from the 1884-1885 edition. Photographs are from *Pomological Possibilities of Texas,* published in 1911 by the Texas Department of Agriculture. The material was made available through courtesy of Mr. William A. Buhler of Victoria, Texas, the University of Texas at Austin, Eugene C. Barker Texas History Center, and the University of Delaware Special Collections Library.

The interest of these nineteenth-century catalogs is not limited to the horticultural content but also the period style of writing by a man who loved words and knew how to use them. He was writing for a business and professional purpose, but he obviously enjoyed the writing itself and he wrote from an extensive vocabulary for precise meaning. Of equally high quality was his talent for illustrative art.

Commissioner of Agriculture Ed R. Kone wrote in his Preface to the 1911 edition of *Pomological Possibilities of Texas:*

"The adaptation of Texas to production of many fruits was recognized by early Spanish settlers, from the indigenous species they found in various parts of the area, including wild grapes, persimmons, pecans, paw-paws, hickory nuts, walnuts, edible berries.... They introduced some European species which they planted about their homes, as did also the Franciscan friars about the missions.

"The first Anglo-American immigrants brought seeds, seedlings and cuttings and established some home gardens, orchards, and vineyards. In later years, knowledge and interest in and practice of horticulture in the State made slow but steady progress to our time, the way being blazed by men of science and enthusiasm, whose names so far have not appeared in any

Texas history, but that will be inscribed in letters of gold on the pages of the real history of Texas that will be written, for they have done more than most of its statesmen to make the State great and happy. Amongst the men to whom I refer, none outranks in length and value of service, knowledge and wisdom, Gilbert Onderdonk."

Fortunately a copy of the Bulletin which Onderdonk had been assigned to write for the Department of Agriculture was preserved by his family. In its fifty-two pages is presented remarkably thorough coverage of cultivation of oranges, figs, strawberries, blackberries, raspberries, dewberries, peaches, grapes, plums, apples, persimmons, apricots, dates, mulberries, pecans, cherries, nectarines, almonds, quinces, walnuts. There is even a section on protective wind breaks, featuring camphor trees, red cedar, and evergreens.

Most interesting was his concern in cautioning the orange grower about the extreme care to be taken in removing fruit from the tree. "No fruit bruises more easily than the orange," he warned, and he urged that a gloved hand be used and that the basket or box should be lined with felt or something similar. "Never handle an orange rudely."

Research finally yielded a copy of the earliest catalog extant from the nursery business which Onderdonk had begun in 1870. Most striking is his complete honesty in what he recommends and what he does not recommend to customers— and why.

Notable, too, was his pioneer venture into the floral business as presented under the Ornamental Department in the catalog. In it he makes the statement, "Texas is the home of the Rose," and that was the first such statement on record. A century later his words would blossom into big business and the famed Tyler Rose Festival.

152-111-5m

TEXAS DEPARTMENT OF AGRICULTURE

BULLETIN

Published Bi-monthly by Texas Department of Agriculture,   Austin, Texas

MARCH-APRIL, 1911   NUMBER 18

POMOLOGICAL POSSIBILITIES OF TEXAS
(REVISED EDITION)

BY
GILBERT ONDERDONK

ED R. KONE,
COMMISSIONER OF AGRICULTURE

Entered as second class matter May 8, 1909, at the postoffice
Austin, Texas, under Act of June 6, 1900.

AUSTIN, TEXAS:
AUSTIN PRINTING CO. PRINTERS
1911

Photographs in the reproduction of the 1888 catalog are from
the Texas Department of Agriculture Bulletin, Number 18,
"Pomological Possibilities of Texas," by Gilbert Onderdonk,
pictured above. All drawings are by Gilbert Onderdonk and are
from his catalogs.

Handbook of Fruits, &c.

FOR

Southern Texas and Louisiana.

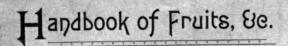

DESCRIPTIVE CATALOGUE

OF THE

Mission Valley Nurseries.

Edition of 1888.

✳

Established
1870.

❋

G. ONDERDONK, Prop'r.

Nursery, Victoria County, Texas.

M. BRUNSWICK & CO., NURSERY SUPPLIES, ROCHESTER, N. Y.

HANDBOOK OF FRUITS, ETC. FOR
SOUTHERN TEXAS AND LOUISIANA (1888)

INTRODUCTION

The Mission Valley Nurseries have been removed from their original location in order to secure better communications. We are now established on the Gulf, West Texas & Pacific Railway at a point ten miles above Victoria, and sixteen miles from Cuero. Here we have secured a station, a post-office, and the best conveniences for daily shipments. We have complete express and freight arrangements, so that we can more promptly serve our patrons.

Our post-office address is now *Nursery, Victoria Co., Texas.*

For thirty-six years the writer has been studying the questions which underlie the horticulture of Southern Texas. At first he had scarcely a precedent to guide him. Little was then known of our horticultural resources. The vast majority of our people then cared but little for any but the grazing interests, and even those who tilled the soil gave their care to two or three staple products.

He who would then suggest that Southern Texas was possessed of even a respectable horticultural capacity was sure to excite a smile of incredulity.

During the last third of a century the writer has done little else than study and experiment for the development of our horticulture. He has planted experimental vineyards containing varieties of every class of grapes known to viticulture. He has planted experimental orchards containing every class of fruit that has seemed to hold out any reasonable hope of success. He has patiently waited for the tests of time to reveal the comparative value of varieties in each department of pomology until he has finally obtained a collection of adapted fruits that he can confidently recommend to our people.

Nor have his experiments in the ornamental department been less exhaustive and complete. One sub-division after another of the general ornamental department has been pursued with studious care and unrelenting energy, until there is now no effect known in the landscape work of the older states for which he has not ascertained practical material to be used in our own climate.

These results have been attained by long and persistent study by many hundreds of carefully conducted experiments and at a very burdensome expense of capital. *Professionally*, he feels that he has attained a highly gratifying success. *Financially*, he has expended a fortune to become properly ready to begin the work of supplying our people. Quite all that he has hitherto done may be regarded as only experimental—a foundation upon which to build the work of coming years.

We have thought best to give this edition more of the character of a hand-book than is usually given to a catalogue. The reader will observe that, in this pamphlet, nothing is recommended except that which has been proven to be of value in our climate, and in every instance a frank intimation is given if there is any drawback against the value of the articles described. A careful examination is invited to every portion of this pamphlet. Every matter stated as fact is based upon the personal experiences of the writer *upon our own grounds.*

After the extraordinary care which we have exercised and the expense we have incurred to become able to *understandingly* serve our people, it can hardly be expected that we shall be called upon to *undersell* other establishments. Many of our patrons have learned the difference between *low priced* trees and really *cheap* ones. Those who require such goods as are supplied by Northern nurseries at very low rates, need not apply to us to compete for low rates. WE DO NOT HANDLE SUCH GOODS, NOR DO WE SELL AT THEIR PRICES!!!

Although our business was at first intended to be only a local one, yet the developments growing out of practical operations in Southern Texas prove to be of importance to other sections also; therefore our business relations have gradually extended to remote regions not anticipated in the beginning of our enterprise. We are better prepared to supply local requirements as well as to better meet the distant demands upon our growing resources. Fortified by such study and experience as could only be prosecuted and attained upon extreme Southern ground—encouraged by the successes of the past, and vastly improved facilities, present and prospective, and the grand army of friends and patrons that have rallied around us, we look forward with large hopes into a cheerful future.

Respectfully,   GILBERT ONDERDONK,

Nursery, Victoria Co., Texas

TO CORRESPONDENTS.—Do not fail to give post-office, county and state, and sign your name *plainly*. Important letters are sometimes signed in such a manner that the name can only be guessed at.

ORDERS.—Do not wait for agents, but send your orders by mail. Write orders on a separate page, and do not mix them up in the body of the letter.

SELECTION OF VARIETIES should be left entirely to us, except in cases where some particular sort is especially required, as we are better acquainted with the varieties, and therefore can make a good selection. When varieties are specified in the order, and the stock of such varieties has become exhausted, we will substitute varieties most resembling those called for, except where substitution is forbidden. In all cases where substitution is forbidden, we will charge retail rates for the plants furnished.

SHIPPING DIRECTIONS should be explicit. When none are given, we forward according to our own judgment; but in no case do we assume any responsibility after delivery to the forwarders.

PACKING CHARGES will be confined to actual cost of material and labor.

PRICES GIVEN relative to deliveries *at the nurseries*. If delivered elsewhere, we shall make a charge to cover cost and risks. Any person or combination of persons who, without intervention of our agents, sends us bills to the amount of $100 or more, will be allowed a deduction of twenty per cent.

MISTAKES will sometimes occur, as we often have to employ inexperienced help, and all our packing is crowded into the space of a few weeks' time. We will correct any mistakes when promptly notified of their occurrence.

REPLACING TREES.— Some customers, after receiving their trees in good order, so neglect or mistreat them as to cause them to die, and afterwards think that we should be responsible for the loss of their trees. We wish it distinctly understood that when a tree or plant has passed beyond our control by being delivered to the purchaser, we cannot be responsible for its treatment or the result. We furnish the trees in good order, and the customer must take care of his own trees, and take his own risk of season, treatment, of any casualties that can interfere with success. It is enough for us to stand our own losses, and we cannot, uncompensated, bear the losses of others. We are not an insurance firm.

We learn that some agents have taken the responsibility of promising to replace any nursery stock their customers may lose. They have done this as an inducement to the customers to deal with them. No customer would sell us cattle, horses or sheep upon such terms, because they all know that *it is not business.* And we want it to be understood and remembered that we make no such contracts. We publish this notice that if these unauthorized promises of an agent are taken it must be understood that they are *not our promises* and that the customer must look to the one with whom he is dealing and *not to us* to fill *his* agreements.

We would like to consider every agents' customers as dealing with us, but when an agent makes contracts of the kind under consideration he is doing something which he has no commission to do for us, and we *will not accept such orders,* although we may sell the agent the goods with which to supply his customers.

TERMS AND REMITTANCES.—Terms cash on or before shipment of package, except when arrangements have been made to the contrary. In cases where prepayment has not been made, and we ship without agreement to the contrary, we shall draw draft to cover the amount upon shipment of goods. Remittances may be made by draft on any reliable business house or bank, or by post-office order or registered letter.

EARLY DELIVERIES.—While our Pear and Apple Trees and Peach Trees of the common Persian race may very properly be removed in November, if the season is an average one, yet our Spanish varieties of Peaches continue to grow much later than those belonging further north. The same may be said of our Plums and Grapes, all of which are especially *southern*, and some other plants. As this makes their season of removal later, we can not, of course, deliver them as early as some nurseries which do not raise our Southern class of trees. Others who even buy much or the *most* of their stock from Northern nurseries, where the season closes much sooner than it does here, can make very early deliveries to customers. When *very early* deliveries are offered, it is a reasonable presumption that the trees do not belong to this region. We do not compete with this class of nurserymen, or *dealers*, on the subject of *early deliveries*. But we *do* deliver as soon as we can handle our trees after they attain the proper condition, and we shall not fail to do so in time to favor the success of our customers.

EXPRESS ARRANGEMENTS have been made with Wells, Fargo & Co. for special rates for all of our customers. Our packing house stands immediately by the platform so that we can ship by every train and make no charge for delivering to the Express Company.

THIS CATALOGUE will be sent free on application.

G. ONDERDONK,
Nursery, Victoria Co., Texas

SELECTION OF GROUND FOR ORCHARDS.

PROMPT DRAINAGE outweighs almost every other consideration—and more especially so for Peaches.

SOIL which is properly drained, and which is good for corn, will generally be found good for Peaches, Plums and Grapes. The same soil should be richer for Apples, Quinces and Pears than for stone fruits. A light sandy loam is best. The lighter the soil, the earlier the trees will bear, and the sooner they will be apt to fail.

EXPOSURE is of some importance. While at the North a plat sloping southward is preferred because it is there desirable to get as much of the sun's influence as possible; yet in our climate the case is different. *We* do not want the first warm rays of the sun to start our trees, as they will then push out the young fruit to be in danger of late frosts. We propose a northern slope *here* as a partial remedy against early growth, but we would yield the question of exposure to any other consideration of importance.

WHEN TO PLANT A TREE.

Trees should not be hurried out of the nursery for planting before they are properly matured for removal. Some people in their desire to plant *early*, overdo the matter by insisting upon their trees being taken up while sap is yet moving too freely. But *after proper maturity*, the sooner they are taken up the better.

In this climate the sap flows, to some extent, all winter. Trees are making roots when there is no outward appearance of growth. We can fix no definite date for planting *here*. Sometimes our trees will do well to handle in November, and sometimes they are hardly fit to dig at Christmas. It depends upon the season. As a rule, we may say that we begin to fill orders as soon as possible after the first *killing* frost, and continue until the planting season is over, which is about March 1st, although the planting in our own grounds continues later. The condition of the tree is of more importance than a few days of time. We never send trees out when it is too late to plant them, and we begin to ship them as soon as they are fit to handle.

WHEN the TREES and PLANTS COME to HAND

if they look fresh they may be planted at once or heeled in moist soil till you are ready to plant. If they are dry enough to be more or less shrunken, then cover the entire tree in a moist soil for a couple of days before planting. But in any case *do not allow the roots to be exposed in the sun or dry wind.*

HOW TO PLANT A TREE.

Many persons plant a tree very much as they would plant a post. Others bestow a large amount of, not only useless, but detrimental labor. We have seen by way of preparation, holes dug from four to six feet square, and as many feet deep, forming in a retentive clay, a receptacle to retain water to the injury if not destruction of the tree. The hole was then nearly filled with bones, rotten wood, and various kinds of manure. Soil was then thrown in to complete the filling, and after this preparation the tree was planted. It would take more space than we can occupy here to delineate the mischief resulting from both of these ways of planting. Don't kill your trees by either neglect or mistaken kindness, and then blame the nurseryman because your trees fail.

The plat should be in a good state of cultivation. Dig the holes large enough to admit the roots without cramping them, and deep enough to admit a couple of inches of surface soil. Cover the bottom with *surface soil* till the tree will stand no deeper than it did in the nursery (except dwarf pear trees, which should be so set that the quince stock is three inches below the surface.) Introduce the roots and earth to each other with the hands, taking care that each root is given its natural position. When the roots are lightly covered pack the earth around them carefully, with any surrounding soil, leaving the surface loose. Use no manure about the roots of a newly planted tree.

IN PLANTING EVERGREENS there are two conditions that must not be disregarded. We remove evergreens with as much safety as we do deciduous trees if they have such roots as ought to be sent out by a nursery. But we do it by regarding the two conditions which we will briefly present: 1st—*Never let the roots of Evergreens become dry before or during the operation of planting.* If obtained from our nursery they will not be dry when they reach the customer. 2d—*Press the earth and roots thoroughly into each other.*

Of course it is to be understood that the operator is to observe the conditions also that are required in planting other trees, especially the one of *letting every root have its natural position.* In planting evergreens I always use to have the earth *beaten* and *tramped* and sometimes *pounded to the roots* in the moist soil. Of course there must be a covering of earth above the root when this pounding is being done so as not to bruise the roots.

DISTANCE FOR PLANTING.

We have planted a peach orchard 16 1/2 feet each way. We see that we should have given more room to the trees. Our latest planting is about 18 by 20 feet, and we never expect to plant a peach orchard nearer on common upland. If I were planting in river bottom I should set the trees 30 by 40 feet. Apple trees in this country become dwarf in their habits and can be set 15 feet by 15. Mariana plums want as much room as peach trees. Other varieties of Plums can be grown at 12 to 15 feet each way. Dwarf pears may be set 12 feet by 12. Standards should be given more room, except LeConte which had better have 30 feet. Our own way of planting pear trees is expressed in our remarks under the head of *pears.*

Our Southern grapes of the Herbemont type should not be set nearer than 10 feet. We set our own 12 feet by 12. Those of the Labrusca type can be set 6 feet by 8. Those of the V. Vinifera may be grown 6 feet by 6. They are often set nearer, but we do not believe in such close planting *here.*

Do not be duped into the fallacious notion of planting trees close enough to shade each other's trunks, but depend upon after treatment which will insure each tree to shade its own trunk. (See remarks on *Pruning Plum, Peach and Apple Trees.*)

HOW TO TREAT AN ORCHARD.

Do not neglect its thorough cultivation. We insist upon cultivation of the soil among fruit trees in this country, notwithstanding the Northern directions in some cases to the contrary. *We do not live in the North.*

Sow no small grain in the orchard! Let the plow go among the trees whenever the growth of weeds and grasses or the condition of the soil requires it. Let the plow run shallow when near enough to the trees to injure the roots, and elsewhere plow as deep as you can. Keep the ground loose, and in all respects in as good condition as it should be for any other crop. If you raise a crop among the trees while they are young, let it be a hoed crop, but plant nothing nearer than within five feet of a tree, and maintain the fertility of the soil by the application of manure. The old chips and rotten wood that collect around the country wood piles make a good manure. A light dressing of ashes is valuable. A cropping of cow peas is good, but in this case some vigilance is required to keep the vines from overrunning the trees.

PRUNING PEACH, PLUM, AND APPLE TREES.

Don't prune your trees to death. Before you begin make up your mind what form of tree you want, and then don't change from one plan to another. We have seen senseless, unintelligent cutting and hacking at trees that was much worse than no pruning at all.

We have peach trees now twenty-six years old still bearing well, that were never pruned, except to keep off the suckers from below the graft. These trees have modified my own views upon the subject of pruning.

Four-Year-Old Satsuma Orange Tree.

Before our trees are sent to our customers, we cut away every side shoot and then cut off the body at from one to two feet from the ground, if the eyes on the trunk of the tree will justify it. For our own planting we cut still closer. The object of this severe pruning is to leave only wood enough to furnish plenty of eyes from which to make the future tree. Some persons object to this severe cutting because they do not understand the matter. In removing a tree we have to deprive it of the majority of its feeders, and the remaining ones cannot well feed the entire original top. By this pruning at the nursery we save, for the customer, half the cost of transportation, make his trees more likely to grow, and secure to him a stronger tree than if the top were not removed. My own peach, plum and apple trees are pruned as follows:

The tree having been cut to a stem, as described above, and properly planted, will put out a large number of sprouts in every direction. To form a low top, select four of these sprouts leading in as many different directions. Move all others and persistently keep any new shoots from supplying the places of those destroyed—training only *the four* shoots selected, and let these four selected branches do pretty much as they please.

If a lateral root from any of these four shoots should hang so low as to be much in the way, I cut it away, but cut no other laterals that are in a vigorous state. If two limbs chafe each other or are likely to do so, I remove one of the offending limbs. If a limb gets badly bruised or broken, I resort to amputation. If trees threaten to interlock limbs with the adjoining ones, I shorten in the interfering boughs. Should a tree be running taller than I wish, I check the tendency by removing the leading boughs. Should one side of the tree be outgrowing the other, I check the excess of the strongest side by shortening its boughs. If trees are treated in this manner, each tree will shade its own trunk. While I train my orchard generally on this plan and thus have low heads—there is occasionally a reason for desiring a tree to become taller and make a rounded head.

In this case, at the first pruning I should retain only one shoot instead of four, shortening the stump back to the sprout selected to stand. As this shoot grows, the lowest side limbs are cut away till the tree has attained its desired height. I do nothing more except to remove interfering limbs or twin sprouts or shorten an occasional bough to preserve the form desired and keep down all suckers from the base of the tree. I remove the suckers at any time when they are discovered, in fact, I prune peach trees at any time that suits my convenience But *pear* trees should not be pruned during the growing season except to rub off young shoots, pinch back leading buds, etc., to preserve the desired form of tree. Dead branches tax the energies of the tree as long as they remain, and therefore should be promptly removed.

Don't keep cutting off the spurs that form on the sides of the trunk and branches. These are preparations for fruit. We have seen the trunks and large limbs trimmed clean of spurs up to near the top of the tree, under a false notion that the good of the tree required it.

We urge the suggestion that whatever growth the peach, plum, pear or apple trees are not allowed to make within a short distance of the ground it will not produce at all. That it is utterly useless and destructive to try to run the trees up to an unnatural height. When peach trees have been treated as we have suggested for about two or three years from planting, they are ready for a careful permanent system of treatment which will improve the size of the fruit.

In January, or before the new growth starts in the Spring, cut away half of each twig of the former year's growth. Let each cut be made just above a leaf bud. The strongest shoots might be cut a little shorter and the weaker ones a trifle less, so as to maintain the symmetry of the tree. This treatment will reduce the number of peaches on the tree, but will vastly increase the size of those remaining. While this treatment is less important here than at the North, yet it may be applied in our orchards with advantage.

That our brief remarks may cover as much ground as possible, I will say that in *all* pruning, whether of fruit trees or flowering shrubs, we must not lose sight of this general principle—viz: *That trees or shrubs that bear their fruits or flowers on wood of the current year's growth should be freely pruned in winter; while those which bear their fruit (or if ornamentals, their flowers,) on wood of the former year's growth should be pruned more sparingly.* The reader will readily see the common sense of this universal rule.

PEACH CULTURE IN SOUTHERN TEXAS.

These chapters were originally written for and published in the *San Antonio Weekly Express.* We were solicited to give them a more permanent form. We published them in our former edition and have concluded to continue them in this issue as embodying our views on this subject.

CHAPTER I

AN OBSTACLE.

In a series upon this subject it is natural to first take a brief view of an obstacle that confronts the cultivator. The first, and one that we will make the subject of this chapter is the

TREE BLIGHT.

In most of the occupied portions of Texas, there are spots of ground upon which cotton and some other plants die out, especially during the early part of the season. All of the grasses seem unaffected by it. Some speak of the ground upon which this blight occurs as "poison soil;" others speak of this singular "dying out" as a result of "*cotton blight;*" and I do not know how many more names have been given to this wide-spread scourge. We have a variety of theories about the cause of this blight. I have my own theory concerning the matter, but think it would be out of place in the series of articles I have now begun. For present purposes it is sufficient to define it as a blight. While it is, in different sections, attributed to different agencies, yet there seems to be sufficient uniformity in its symptoms and effects in different localities to lead us to presume upon the identity of the scourge. This blight is quite sure to kill every apple and pear tree and every grape vine which it attacks, and sometimes destroys peach trees, rose bushes, and a great variety of trees are killed by it. I have seen the trees of a whole orchard—one by one, in regular succession—yield to its withering power.

TO DETECT THE BLIGHT BEFORE PLANTING,

plant cotton or ground peas on the spot. If either of these remain uninjured at the close of the first season, then there is no tree blight in the plot, and you may safely set your trees. But suppose one has already set an orchard and afterwards discovers that he has located it in an infected spot,

IS THERE A REMEDY?

I once found that this blight had begun its ravages on my vineyard. Wood was abundant near by and the affected spot was small, so I built a large fire, gradually moving and extending it, till the whole spot had been heated to a redness. I threw into the fire everything combustible that was on the spot. I went ahead of every sign of blight and burnt vines that seemed to be unaffected. This proved efficient. I replanted the burned plot and had no more blight there to this day. This was twenty-two years ago. So I may safely say that I cured this spot of "*blight*," or rather killed the myriads of insects that caused it. It is to be regretted that we have not a state entomologist to study up such cases and learn some practical mode of destruction, so that they could be dealt with where the pest extends to large patches. It generally appears on a too large scale to burn out in this manner, and then the best way I know of is to seek another spot upon which to set a new orchard. I have in my mind a case in which the owner of a blighted orchard set a second orchard of two hundred trees, only a couple of hundred yards distant. In this case the blight ceased after killing about a hundred trees, and the remainder, like the new planting, lived to a good old age without becoming affected. In our next we will notice the question of drainage.

CHAPTER II

DRAINAGE AND SOILS.

For convenience and brevity and to avoid repetition, we will treat together the questions of soil and drainage. Defective drainage is the most serious obstacle in the way of peach culture. Whatever importance may properly be attached to questions of soil or aspect, yet, in fruit culture, the question of drainage outweighs every other consideration, and more especially so in peach culture. Peach trees cannot endure wet feet for a great length of time. I shall probably find no better place to say that injudicious irrigation has killed many a promising tree.

For peach trees it is not sufficient that the water can run off—but it must run off promptly. Many a spot of ground which would be considered well drained for corn or cotton, or small grain, will nevertheless retain water too long for peach trees. If water stands on the surface a few hours in a peach orchard, it is doing mischief to the roots of the trees.

If the soil is that kind of sandy loam that retains so much water as to remain boggy long after rain, that is a grave objection to it for a peach orchard. Such a soil may be, and generally is, splendid for the growth of the trees under ordinary circumstances; but in a very wet season its power of retaining so much water is often fatal to the trees. I have seen this result even where the surface drainage would be called good. An orchard in such a place may do well for a dozen years and then be destroyed by a rainy spell, which makes the ground boggy for a month. But if you have a light sandy loam, that has both good surface drainage and a good under drainage, then you have a perfect spot for a peach orchard.

It has been observed by many that the clay subsoil, immediately below their sandy loam, is very uneven, so that if the surface soil were removed the clay would present a surface like what we call "hog wallow" prairie. If you have such a subsoil of clay it will hold water a long time in the little basins formed by its uneven surface, and a long wet spell is sometimes so nearly equal to a continued overflow that the peach roots may be so far injured that when the drought of the following year comes along, the trees have not sufficient nourishment from the few remaining sound roots to support them, yield to the power of the drought and die. Many are so far injured by the water of the clay basins that they do not even wait for a dry spell to die in. There are many dead and dying orchards from this cause all over Southern Texas. Many orchards with a pretty fair drainage are so far injured at the roots by an unusually wet spell that in the following spring the trees shed much or even all of their fruit and perhaps even maintain a sickly yellow for a season till new root feeders have formed sufficiently to properly sustain the trees.

There is much of this kind of clay sub-soil (with clay basins) in Southern Texas. I do not want to be understood to say that this clay is not good for peach trees—on the other hand I believe it is good for them when not formed into clay basins. Nor do I want to be understood to say that the soil above this clay is not good, for I believe it is good when properly drained. But, at the risk of some repetition, I will say that it is the clay basin which hold the water that do the mischief wherever these basins exist.

Where one is compelled to plant upon such a plot, or not at all, there is a simple but not always cheap remedy.

An underdrain, three feet deep under each row, will preserve the orchard. Of course this underdrain should precede the planting of the orchard, or it could not be under each row. But if the orchard is already planted upon ground that has this defect, it would be much improved by an underdrain between each row as the best that can yet be done.

Of course these underdrains must have a good outlet. Where tiles cannot reasonably be obtained, a good substitute for tiling can be made of plank. Two six-inch planks nailed together at their edges so that a cross section would resemble an Λ,would answer the purpose. The filling of the ditch should all be of the surface soil, leaving the clay from the ditch to be mixed with the surface soil of the plot.

It seems to be the case that wherever we have the red clay as a sub-soil, it usually lies so even that no clay basins are formed. Even if they exist in *such clay* I think that it will hardly hold water long enough to prove a serious matter. This clay also seems favorable to peach culture. The soils upon it are, I believe, generally of a firm nature and seldom boggy. If the surface drainage of such a plot is even tolerably good, it is a good site for a peach orchard. I have, on such ground, trees over twenty years old and still productive.

Many persons prepare for tree planting by digging enormous holes into the clay sub-soil, filling them with earth, manure, etc., and thus imitate the natural clay basins to which I have referred, and they are quite apt to reach such results as the clay basins give, only they reap them more promptly and with greater certainty. We here refer the reader to our remarks under the title "How to Plant a Tree."

Reviewing the combined question of soil and drainage, I would say that I prefer sandy loam for peach trees if the drainage is complete. But I must insist that no excellence of soil or aspect can compensate for defective drainage. So if I had to express the largest amount of truth on this subject in a single sentence, I should say that the best-drained soil, if reasonably good, is the best place for a peach orchard.

The summits of elevated places where no water can flow from other ground afford good sites for peach orchards. The tops of live oak hills are especially favorable.

CHAPTER III.

In writing a series of articles upon this subject, it would be desirable if we could examine in detail, every principle and practice that bears upon the subject. But this would involve an outlay of time which I cannot now spare. I hope, however, at some future time, to do myself the pleasure of bringing before the public, in a convenient form, the conclusions reached from experience and observation in Western Texas during the last thirty-five years. But for the present I must be contented as a survey of only the landmarks that define the way of the most successful peach culture in our general section. We now come to a department of the subject which is too often overlooked— I mean the questions relation to

CLIMATIC ADAPTATION.

It is recognized by intelligent minds everywhere that within each separate department of both animal and vegetable life there are distinct constitutional differences. For example—in the animal kingdom when we look at the bovine department we see a large number of different breeds all under one general name of cattle. Yet these different breeds, or as we correctly express it, these different *varieties* of cattle have qualities and capacities very widely differing. We find that some varieties are better adapted to certain purposes, or section, or climate, than another. These differences are found to have become constitutional.

The same is true of horses, of hogs, of sheep, and even of men. It is noticably true in the bear family. Each general region has its own peculiar type of bears. The grizzly of the Rocky Mountains never invades the hills and valleys of Texas. The white bear of the polar regions, if given the freedom of our forest, would not live a week in our Summer.

If we turn our attention to the vegetable kingdom we find differences analagous to those in animal life. Let the farmer of Southern Texas send to Minnesota for oats, or wheat or corn with which to plant his fields, and while, perhaps, in an exceptional season, he may reap a fair crop, yet he will generally fail. While some crops, which can be quickly made, may here encounter, during their short time of growth, conditions so resembling their season of growth in their natural habitat as to suffer little or no deterioration by removal to a different climate, yet such products as require a long period of time to reach perfection are quite likely to reveal a constitutional want of adaptation when removed considerably southward.

As fruit trees must be exposed to all the vicissitudes of climate through the entire year, it follows, as a natural consequence, that they must be subject to any effects which the climate is capable of producing. Thus habits of growth, habits of bearing, and the durability of the tree, are all affected by climate. In cases of some kinds of trees the tax upon their resources is so great as to undermine their constitution and hurry them to an early decay. In fact, the history of the subject, and results of universal observation of students in this department, have crystalized into the acknowledged theory the world over, that nature has set bounds for each variety of fruit.

And here it is well to observe that the great peach family has been divided by the Grand Architect of nature, into races as distinct from each other as are the different races of men. And while each race of men can become adapted to the conditions of the other, we find that this is not to a great extent true of the different races of the peach. Each has its proper zone of habitation, and when we carry them beyond it their very constitutions rebel against the change and they refuse to give us success.

The Persian race, belonging in the higher latitudes, should not be brought below the limits assigned by nature.

While latitude is conceded to be a general guide in estimating the possible habitation of any product, yet physical geographists have found that from modifying causes the line of equal temperature, which we call isothermal lines, make important variations from the lines of latitude, and that these isothermal lines, with the modifications resulting from different degrees of humidity, determine the natural places of habitation of not only the fruits, but each form of vegetable life, and right here

A GREAT PRINCIPLE IN NATURE

is often overlooked. We should keep in mind the great principle or rule of nature, that each vegetable product is more vigorous as we approach its polar limit of perfect development. When we pass its limit of perfect development we find marks of deterioration from the rigors of climate. In cases of fruits the constitution and longevity of the trees are impaired, although perfection in fruit may be obtained to the polar limit of existence. Thus in peach culture we find that as we approach the northern limit of this fruit, while the quality of the fruit is fully maintained, yet such weakness has the stock of trees attained in comparison with those of forty years ago, that it often excites the inquiries of old observers.

And when this Persian race, even if possessing all of its original strength, is brought to our zone where it is not only unadapted, but is subject to the principle just named, we see a double cause of its failure.

And here let us recall

ANOTHER PRINCIPLE

that has been too much lost sight of by our Northern nurserymen, and it is one that cannot be denied, and we are sure that its non-observance has done quite as much, perhaps, as their climate to undermine the constitution of their trees.

While it is doubtful whether grafting or budding, when properly done, interfere with the constitution of a tree, yet it is true that the *seeds* grown upon a grafted tree are reduced in vigor and will not produce as strong trees as seeds grown upon seedlings. When seedling orchards became scarce at the North, the nurserymen there planted such seeds as they could get, which were generally seed of grafted trees. They have continued this process so long that an additional degeneration has overtaken their entire stock of peach trees. And so great is the deterioration from the different causes that most of their fine peach orchards fail at from eight to eleven years from the date of planting. *And yet many of our people continue to buy peach trees from that degenerated supply!* We will follow up this matter in our next.

CHAPTER IV

In our last we showed some of the ways in which the whole Northern race of peach trees became degenerated and deplored the extent to which that degenerated race has been supplying orchards for Southern Texas. Let us now turn our attention to another phase of this matter.

Having been grown so long at the North, and although degenerated in vigor and longevity by its Northern residence, yet the peach became in a certain sense, acclimated there, and in fact there was established a strain peculiar to the climate in which it has so long existed. It would be a natural inference that when a stock of trees had been degenerated by being carried too far North for a healthy existence, that to again bring it Southward would restore the lost vigor. But it has been found in actual practice, that after the degree of acclimation which the peach attained there, it was subject to the

CONVERSE PRINCIPLE

that while fruits generally are improved by being carried toward their polar limit of perfect development—that they are deteriorated by being carried toward their equatorial limit. And yet our people have been getting their trees from Nashville, Bloomington, and even points still further North, to be planted in Southern Texas! and when they find their trees unproductive they wonder (! ! !) and cry out "*what can be the matter with the trees?*" and at once conclude that this is not a peach country, without reflecting that they have been doing such violence to the principles of vegetable life that they thus secured their own failure.

But right here some one will say that he planted trees from Mobile or New Orleans or Eastern Texas—or perhaps from a nursery in his own neighborhood—and yet has experienced the same results. And such a one will ask why he also failed as completely as the neighbor who got his trees from a Northern nursery. Surely there is a reason for his failure. I will try to point out the reason if "poison soil" borers, or want of drainage, or his own neglect had anything to do with it, for either of these could have killed an orchard whether of suitable or unsuitable trees. This brings us again to the matter of

UNSUITABLE TREES.

In the first place we will note that some of our Texas nurserymen buy a part of their trees from Northern nurseries, and in such cases the customer may as well have sent to the North and got his trees from first hands. In the next place I will say that I do not know of a nursery anywhere in the South, except our own, that does not make up nearly their entire supply of trees from this same degenerate race that their Northern brethren use. This is the whole thing in a nutshell. It does not mend the matter to say that the yellow St. John originated at New Orleans, or Lipscomb's prize is a seedling from Montgomery county, Texas, or that this or that variety originated in Georgia, Alabama, Mississippi or Texas, as long as the fact remains that it belongs to that unadapted stock of which we are complaining. A tree having been grown here from seed is no proof of the race to which it belongs any more than that because a man was born in a stable he should be regarded as a horse. I have seedlings originated from the Persian race on my own premises, from seed grown here by myself, and these seedlings show every sign of non-adaptation peculiar to the race to which they belong.

I do not say that by continuing for a long time, through many generations of trees, that a final acclimation would not result. I believe it would. But I do say that the nature of the Persian race or its constitutional want of adaption to our climate cannot be eradicated through the seed in only a few generations of trees in a genial climate. It is more deeply seated than that. Another may say that he has even raised his own trees and grafted or budded them himself, and yet his results are no better

79

than when he bought from a Northern source. I will answer such a one with a statement that general experience has proved that when we graft a tree we not only propagate the *variety* of fruit, but the variety of *tree* with its *entire habits*, except in cases of dwarfing.

When I bud from a plum tree upon peach stocks, I get simply a plum tree with peach roots, and of the very variety of plum which I grafted from, whether early, late, large or small.

When I bud from a peach tree that is diseased, I find that the disease is propagated with the tree. When I bud from a peach tree of the Persian race that will not here, once in ten years, produce more than twenty-five peaches at a crop, I uniformly find that I have thus propagated trees that only bear in the same way, and that show all the points of weakness exhibited by the tree which I budded from.

When I bud from a tree of the Southern Chinese race, or from one of the Spanish race that our people call native seedlings—one that is a heavy bearer—I find that I have produced trees that are as productive as the trees from which my buds were taken. If this were not so why should we bud at all?

In general terms (except in cases of dwarfing), I propagated by budding the same thing from which my buds were taken with the entire habits practically continued in the product, very seldom finding that the stock has any very marked effect upon the resulting tree. So I feel very safe in saying to the reader who budded from the unadapted tree, that he surely would, and did, find that he had propagated all the defects of the tree from which he budded, and no right to expect any other result. Of course, then he would fail with them just in the same way as he did with his Northern trees. Here I wish to point out to the reader

AN UNEXPECTED DEVELOPMENT.

While I have varieties of the Persian race that have been budded in extreme Southern Texas for more than thirty years, and others of the same race that have been thus propagated here ever since the introduction to the public, and while I cannot see that these varieties seem to be any more productive or any better adapted here than at the beginning of their culture here, yet I have been surprised to learn that when these trees so produced here have been carried, even only a short distance Northward, they have proven much better bearers than trees of the same varieties that have been raised further northward. While I did not foresee this development, it is now very easy to refer it to a general law which I have already stated, but which can scarcely be too often repeated in this connection, viz: that fruit trees are improved by being carried toward their polar limit of perfect development. This fact is of great value to those occupying the belt of country that lies just below the line of success with the Persian race, and even further North. Upon this principle we have established our nurseries as far South as it is practical to carry on general nursery operations.

In my next I propose to present, at least, a partial remedy against the disappointments in fruit culture that have followed every effort of so many enterprising men in Southern Texas.

CHAPTER V.

We may as well pause here, and take a chapter for a word of explanation. We have had it suggested to us that although nature has divided the general peach family into five races, yet that our *terms* by which we distinguish these races from each other are "*arbitrary.*"

We reply that in speaking of *things* we must have *terms* by which to designate them, or we should be involved in frequent confusion or cumbersome circumlocution. It is a poor thing that has not about it enough that is sufficiently distinct to suggest a name for *itself.* If it has this then the name is *not arbitrary.*

We speak of the *Persian* race because we can readily trace it back to Persian origin.

We speak of the *Spanish* race because, although it is probably of final Persian origin, yet have not been able to trace it beyond its Spanish possessors, and if we should, still it seems to have taken its distinct characteristics in Spanish hands.

We speak of the *Northern Chinese* race because it is traced directly to China, and because it is more Northern in its habitation than any other race of Chinese peaches.

We speak of *Southern Chinese* race because it has a more Southern position in its natural habitation.

We speak of the *Peen To* race because we understand that the term signifies *flat peach* in the Chinese language.

We do not say that these are the best possible terms by which these races of peaches should be distinguished from each other, but for the present, until better authority shall have given names, we shall designate these races according to the above nomenclature.

CHAPTER VI.

In former numbers I have given attention to some of the causes of the failure in peach culture in Southern Texas. I have endeavored to point out that while poison soil, peach borers, defective drainage, and neglect had each borne their part, and either one may effect the success of an orchard, yet that the grand cause of dissatisfaction, disappointment and failure was that our people have been planting trees from a race not suited to our climate. The question very naturally arises:

WHAT IS THE REMEDY?

One part of our remedy lies in not planting trees of this class. Another part in using the Southern races that are found to be adapted to our region. We will mention them separately.

FIRST—THE SPANISH RACE.

We already have a hardy race of trees that suits our climate well, and is very productive. It has been cultivated in Southern latitudes till it has become thoroughly adapted to Southern climates on the lower border of the zone in which the peach has been considered possible. The vigor of this race from Spain has not been diminished by its treatment in Mexico and Texas during its long existence here. If, before its introduction by the Catholic missionaries, it needed to be established into a distinct race, yet its propagation here for more than two centuries of time has given to the trees all the characteristics of a separate and distinct race from that now in general cultivation by the nurseries of the United States and Europe.

It has extended in the extreme South, from Florida to Mexico. It has made its way up the Mississippi and other streams. It has overrun Texas and every part of Mexico where it will flourish.

Everywhere the trees have been recognized as hardy seedlings, which, although not claiming the highest excellence in quality, were nevertheless successful growers and fine bearers, often developing choice varieties. They are now known all over Southern Texas as the most reliable race of peach trees that have been generally tested by our settlers. Surely we shall hardly find a better foundation upon which to base improvements.

When the Persian race was disseminated among our people, some of them grafted from it upon these vigorous Spanish stocks, thinking that the superior strength of the stock would be imparted to the newly made tree, and thus they would get the fine qualities of the Persian race combined with the hardy character of the Spanish. But, however reasonable this appeared, yet every one knows how this expedient failed (as we represented in a former number), not because the new trees were grafted, but because they were developed into trees of the Persian race.

About thirty-seven years ago I began to study this race of seedlings. I saw how hardy productive and long-lived it was, and embraced the belief that it could be vastly improved. I spared no pains to learn what could be done towards

THE DEVELOPMENT OF THE SPANISH RACE.

The beginnings of an enterprise are almost always feeble. In its early stages it generally progresses slowly. In this respect, this enterprise proved no exception to the general rule, and this one of developing a valuable list of fruit, from even such a beginning, would be a life-long undertaking.

Then came the war, with all its crushing calamities—years of absence in military life, of distracting thought, of scattering material and dissipating capital, terminating in a shipwreck of quite all that had been accomplished. But perseverance is a mighty agent of success.

Thousands of seedings were fruited in the hope of finding, here and there one of standard merit. Such as appeared valuable were preserved, while all the rest were sent to the brush pile to make room for another installment of seedlings to be treated in a similar manner.

This plan has been continued to the present day, and has developed some choice varieties. These were all grafted for preservation. Meanwhile, valuable seedlings were found in the many seedling orchards all over Southern Texas. Cuttings were taken from these and preserved by grafting. Large experimental orchards were made up, consisting of the varieties collected from Spanish seedlings of Texas. Time was then allowed to test the comparative value of the varieties in the collection. Careful comparisons of the varieties in these experimental orchards were made from year to year, and enabled the rejection of those less valuable and the retention of such as were found to be superior; and thus, finally, a revised list was the result of the protracted enterprise.

This, in connection with similar efforts in other departments, made our premises little else than a horticultural experimental station, at our own expense, for many years. But it seemed a necessary prelude to our future enterprises, and we adhered to the policy till we have reached a large part of the results at which we were aiming. And here let me say regarding the advice to plant seed in order to secure a reliable orchard, that it must be remembered that while it is true that the orchards so raised from our native seed will be hardy and productive, yet it is also true that the greatest number of such trees will not prove to be varieties of merit. But if you want a good orchard of good peaches then buy grafted trees of acclimated varieties such as can be got at the Mission Valley Nurseries and you will have all the hardiness and productiveness of the native seedling, combined with the quality of the finer varieties.

CHAPTER VII.

In former numbers we have considered the fact of the unreliable character of the varieties of the Persian race when planted in extreme Southern Texas. We refer to the fact that at tide water, and for some distance toward the interior, the Persian race is worthless—that as we go farther we reach a belt in which they usually produce sparingly and occasionly bear a good crop, but, on the whole, are so unreliable as to disappoint and discourage the cultivator, while still higher in the interior these varieties give reasonable success, and yet in the regions still beyond this they are considered successful.

We observe that where these varieties are a partial success these seasons of non-productiveness follow mild winters when the isothermal lines lie temporarily further northward than usual; and conversely that the productive seasons for this strain follow our severe winters; when the isothermal lines lie more southward. And when we compare these last two facts with the fact that this race generally succeeds in a more rigid climate, we have a solid line of facts that combine in a very marked confirmation of our theory that the degree of success or failure which is obtained with this Northern race, is not a question of soil, but a *result of climate.*

We have presented the native peaches, or, as we have chosen to define them, the Spanish race, as a sound basis upon which to construct our orchards in Southern Texas. But, while we recede from nothing which we have claimed for our Spanish race, yet we must concede that there is one want which it does not yet supply. It has given us no extra early varieties. What shall we plant then to secure extra early peaches? This is a real difficulty. While we shall probably develop much earlier varieties from our natives than we now have, yet that prospect does not give us a present supply. As a partial remedy we propose some varieties of

THE SOUTHERN CHINESE RACE

While writers upon the origin of the peach universally state that "the peach originated in Persia" yet I do not think there is any way of proving that China may not be claimed also as a primitive home.

While the Western nations carried the peach westward from the place of its origin and have made wonderful improvements upon the original yet the Chinese made developments of, or discovered types very different from anything we have seen in the West. They seem to have found originally, or else developed both northern and southern types which differ so widely from each other, that it seems hardly proper to define these lines of difference as those of mere strains but rather allow them the real prominence they present and admit their identity as races.

The Southern Chinese race seems perfectly at home all over Southern Texas. It is productive, even after the coldest winters, and the entire race, so far as we are acquainted with it, is earlier than the earliest Spanish variety. This race then is a valuable acquisiton to a region where the early varieties of the Persian type are so far unsuccessful as to be unprofitable. The developments of this race among us have only just begun, and yet they are such as to excite the liveliest interest. Already we have five choice varieties, besides others not yet disseminated, making a succession from the last days of May to the Spanish varieties. We have now a lot of seedlings from which we have every reason to hope to obtain a variety to rival in earliness the Alexander. While the *Peen To* race has thus far, proven itself too far North with us, yet we may hope that some of its seedlings may prove late bloomers and be found adapted to our region as well as among the oranges, lemons and pineapples of Florida.

When we reflect what has been done with certain strains of the Persian race in the line of developing early varieties and remember the great length of time that has been required for its accomplishment, and then consider what a very short period has elapsed since our first acquaintance with the Southern Chinese race, we may well expect that at no remote day we shall exceed any limit of earliness that has ever been proposed.

While the Northern Chinese race generally are very successful in Central and Northern Texas, yet the coast region is below their proper zone, and most varieties of this type are not successful here except in special localities where local modifications enable them to succeed.

CHAPTER VIII.

REPRODUCTION OF VARIETIES OF FRUIT FROM SEED.

In Southern Texas, among persons whose notions have not been corrected by experiences, it is a very common mistake to suppose that if they plant seed from good fruit only they will be sure of producing only trees that will bear fruit equal to, if not identical with, the fruit from which the seeds were taken. They think that varieties of fruit are reproduced from seed with as much certainty as are varieties of potatoes or any garden vegetable.

However amusing this notion may seem to those who know better, yet it is a more serious matter to those who are going to risk their understanding of this principle in the orchard they are about to plant, instead of procuring improved trees from some reliable nursery.

In 1858 I purchased the entire crop from a certain favorite peach tree. Reliable improved trees could not then be procured in this country. My design was to secure something desirable from it, and I expected to obtain a few individual trees from the lot that would be an approximate reproduction of the original, or a possible improvement. I brought to fruiting about one hundred and fifty trees from this lot of seed. Twenty of them bore a marked resemblance to the original tree, the fruit differing in size and season of ripening. A few did not differ in any perceptible way. One was a decided improvement upon the original from which I took the seed the fruit being more uniformly large and excellent. This one I named Onderdonk's Favorite. The other one hundred and thirty-two, which came from this lot of seed, presented almost every possible variety of character and appearance. So my result was one very choice variety, a few rather desirable, some rather ordinary and the greatest number positively mean. And yet my success in this experiment with seed is greater than I should obtain in one experiment out of twenty. Out of another lot of sixty seedlings I obtained one worth grafting from. Another lot of five hundred gave only one from which I was willing to graft. Another lot of five hundred seedlings yielded two which I considered worth grafting from. Another lot of three hundred seedlings gave one valuable variety. Another lot of two thousand seedlings gave none that I was willing to admit as worthy of adding to my list of valuable varieties. I planted plum seeds from a large number of fine plums. I got about five hundred varieties from this lot of seed, and not one variety in the whole lot had any considerable resemblance to any variety from which I planted seed. And yet in all of these cases I used seed from choice, selected fruit, produced over thirty-five hundred seedlings and obtained only six really very choice varieties. It is true that there were sixty or possibly a hundred trees of fruit which, although not good enough to graft from, were nevertheless good enough to preserve as fruit trees. But, while this was the case, yet the largest number of them ranged from common to miserably mean. And who wants to bring thirty-five hundred peach trees to bear in his orchard to get even a hundred good ones, while he will have thirty-four hundred ranging in quality from common to mean? supplying fruit for six weeks of time, when a hundred trees, every one bearing good fruit and ripening in succession for six months in the year, can be bought at the nursery for twenty dollars.

"But why," the incredulous will ask, "can we not get from our fruit seed the same varieties as those from which the seed were taken?" The sensible reader will ask if the laws of nature are not regular and certain. Then why this wide variation in fruit resulting from seed taken from the same tree? I will answer.

If the reader will examine a peach blossom, or the blossom of any fruit tree, he will see in the center, standing distinct and alone, a tall, stem-like looking object with a peculiar termination at the top. The central object is called the pistil. The upper termination is called the stigma, and is the female organ of reproduction for this particular bloom. Arranged around the pistil may be seen a large number, perhaps twenty-five or more, thread-like organs called stamens, each terminating at the top with a flat cushion-like appendage called the anther. The anther may be regarded as the male organ of reproduction. The anther holds the pollen, which, to the naked eye, appears like a very fine dust; but when examined under a magnifier of sufficient power each particle presents to the eye the most delicate form.

Now if no pollen from any anther should ever reach the stigma of the pistil of any given bloom, then no fruit could ever result from that bloom. But whenever any of the pollen from any of the anthers of any bloom is lodged upon the stigma of the bloom, the ovary, which constitutes the lower part, becomes fertilized, and the seed of the future begins to develop. The variety of pollen fixes the variety of the coming seed. The fruit surrounding the seed, is, in a botanical sense, only a matured ovary, and exists only to secure the development of the seed. It is not realized by every one that the fruit that we do highly prize, and for which we cultivate the tree, is, after, all only an incidental result in the production of the seed for which we care so little.

In the above analysis we see that the *fruit* resulting from the fertilization of each particular bloom, is, in a proper sense, only a developed portion of the tree upon which it grows, and, therefore is not changed in variety by the character of the pollen which fertilized the seed enclosed in it, while the *seed* in accordance to the fixed laws of reproduction, necessarily partakes of the peculiarities imparted by the pollen by which it was brought into being.

If every stigma were fertilized with pollen from the stigma's own tree, then the trees resulting from such seed would reproduce exactly the same variety of fruit. But there are circumstances that combine to defeat this result. The stigma and pollen of a bloom not being both in a stage of maturity for fertilization at the first opening of the flower, constitutes an important condition. The existence of other trees with their burdens of pollen within fertilizing distance constitutes another condition no less important. Then the busy bees—the myriads of insects that buzz from flower to flower, and even the passing breeze that floats by the tiny bloom—each bear their own portion of the minute particles of the fertile pollen, and although without design mingle them in an untold number of combinations, scattering them in countless directions to distances little imagined by the casual observer, and establishing modifications as numberless as variety itself.

CHAPTER IX.

We have endeavored to show that if we of Southern Texas do, for some special reason, plant any trees of the Persian type, yet they should never comprise the bulk of our orchards. I will now specify under just what circumstances I should plant trees of this type. For while the stock of trees of this race is especially degenerated when removed to our climate, yet it does contain many very choice varieties of fruit which we can never excel and some of which we have not equaled.

Those of us who live below the line of possible success with the northern varieties have no present remedy beyond the present development of the Spanish and Chinese races of peaches, except that we migrate to regions of a more rigid climate. But while we of the Southern counties have not a present remedy, yet we may well hope for a future remedy not far distant. The Persian type has probably quite reached its limit of earliness. While it has for centuries been subject to the improvements of horticulturists, giving it time for the fullest development, yet we have but just begun with the Southern races. And when we consider our improvements during the last quarter of a century we can cast a cheerful glance into the future, and easily expect rapid progress to mark the way of the years to come.

But many of our readers live within the zone of partial success with the Persian race.

Some who are thus situated have very high ground upon which they could plant an orchard. Let such remember that every two hundred and fifty feet of elevation attained is equivalent to a degree of latitude. This is a valuable item to them. If they are willing to cultivate an uncertain crop for the sake of its luxury when it "does hit," then let them plant some tree of early northern varieties—Beatrice, Louise and Alexander, Rivers, or others of the same season. Sometimes they will get a fair crop of extra early peaches, and very often they will get a few peaches, while sometimes they will get no fruit at all. But if they insist upon extra early peaches—earlier than we have named of the Spanish and Chinese races, then the above is the best that we can do without migrating to a country of cooler winters. But if they *do* plant such varieties in the low regions of Southern Texas, let them go into it with the understanding that it is an uncertain venture, in which only partial success is even possible; and let them remember the principle which teaches that they should get trees which were raised more southward than their orchards if possible.

While the varieties of the Persian race will not bear an average of twenty peaches to the tree in my own grounds, yet if I were located seventy miles further northward I would plant moderately of the extra early varieties of the Persian race, and a few of the best later varieties, while I would principally rely upon Spanish varieties, and even if I lived in the regions of success with the Persian race, yet I should plant largely of the Spanish race as experiments in different sections of higher latitudes show these varieties improved by being carried northward. As the preface to a work should always be written after the work is completed, so in the present case, that which might have appeared in the preface must be presented as a conclusion.

There are many matters of interest properly included in the general subject which I have been considering. It would be pleasant to examine many details that could be named, but concerning which I have been silent. It is one thing to carefully survey an entire region, and quite another to simply pass through it and point out the land marks by which one must define a general way. And this last has been my policy in dealing with the outlines of a subject that, if amply considered, would fill a large volume. I have done little else than present such general principles as seem to lie at the bottom of success of peach culture in Southern Texas.

I have not the presumption to claim to "know all about" this subject, but for thirty-seven years I have been studying it with all the light that has been shed upon it by my own reason, observation, experience and the help of the vast number of men who have each contributed their share in the mighty work of developing the vast slumbering pomological resources of Southern Texas. Our region contains plenty of men who, if they had given themselves to the same work, could have explored the same field with as much energy and faithfulness, and, quite likely, with earlier and more thorough results. And our region is also full of men at the present hour who have reached quite the same general conclusions that we have drawn in this series of articles. But horticulture has not been their profession; therefore they naturally pursue each his own special object in life.

I should be dull, indeed, if, after devoting my life to horticultural subjects, I had not gained a respectable amount of information in the line of my profession. But my readers, *I do not know it all*. I am learning every day. I now learn more in one year then I used to learn in ten. I now often wonder at my own clumsiness in certain departments only a decade back in my history, and if the developments of the future are to keep pace with those of the past (and why not?) then if I live another decade I shall look back with wonder upon the status of our improvement in 1888. In each special branch of horticulture, as in other departments of human enterprise, there is a wide room for improvement. So I do not ask the reader of these chapters to regard them as infallible. They are only the present result of my best information from all sources after a patient study of a little more than a third of a century.

OUR LISTS OF PEACHES.

We have rearranged our lists of peaches that they may be in better harmony with the progress that has been made in Southern peach culture. The developments of the different races of the peach in our low latitudes, and the comparative position which each is found to occupy upon a scale of isothermal lines, seem to require that we should not ignore the distinctions that have been made by nature, and which so persistently force themselves upon our attention by their practical relations to an important department of our business life.

The development of the Spanish and Chinese races of peaches promises vast results to Southern pomology. We have reached that point in the study of peach culture for this region that we recognize a very unexpected amount of difference in the very narrow zones that succeed each other from the coast country to the mountains. Our communications are extending—our trade has ceased to be purely local—and we realize that we must meet the growing demands of more extended intercourse. We have, therefore, decided upon separate lists of peaches to accommodate climate conditions of customers in different sections.

Some of the boundaries given upon the isothermal chart may need correction, but we are satisfied that we quite correctly state the relative position of these races. While all careful students of physical geography must admit that on account of the unequal distribution of heat during the extremes of the year, the isothermal lines of the world generally are not a sure guide to estimating the possible productions of a climate, yet for our purposes, in speaking of the products of Texas, such are the conditions that we may take these lines as a general guide in our remarks about our peach culture.

We refer the reader to the report of the United States Commissioner of Agriculture for 1887. Page 648 to 651.

THE PERSIAN RACE occupies the most Northern position of any race of peaches. It extends to the Northern limits of peach culture, and seems, in some varieties to succeed well down to about the isothermal of 65, while under the modifying influence of local causes it even runs down to the line of 68. And a very few varieties have, under the most favorable and rare conditions, given fair partial success as low down as the line of 70. But we have not heard of any of this race being found so well adapted as to be regularly productive in any general locality as far down as this last named limit.

This race was brought from Persia to Italy during the reign of the Emperior Claudius. It was introduced into Great Britain about 1550, and to the American colonies about 1680. They are all late bloomers, and cannot carry their foliage through the growing season of the Southern portion of the belt in which they are cultivated. This race includes the varieties usually propagated by the Northern nursery men and composes the bulk of the Northern orchards.

We have found the following varieties among those best adapted to the Southern portion of the zone of this race. Except in river bottoms, in the immediate vicinity of a body of water sufficient to relieve to some extent the aridity of our atmosphere, even partial success must not be expected with this list on or below the isotherm of 70.

Our nurseries are about in this line, and these varieties are not profitable here. We confidently send these varieties Northward, especially to positions three or four hundred feet higher than we are. But we always regret to have orders for them to go Southward, except to one whom we know has a favorable position for them. We have varieties that at our premises are practically worthless, and yet are a fair success only a short distance above us. We are upon a line where a few miles North or South make an important difference. We are bringing these questions nearer to a point every year.

PERSIAN LIST OF PEACHES

Prices—30 cents each; $3 per dozen; $20 per hundred.

Alexander—Above medium, highly colored in clay soils, less colored in light soils; flesh greenish white, very juicy, adheres to the seed. Maturity May 9th to 20th. The earliest variety in cultivation.

Amelia—Very large, conical, white, nearly covered with crimson; juicy, sweet, of high flavor. Too tender for market but splendid for home use.

Beatrice—Small to medium; deep red; good quality; matures immediately after Alexander, May 20.

Bexar—Very large; white; red cheek; looks very much like Old Mixon Free, but is three weeks later. A seedling from San Antonio, Texas.

Elmira—Large, white, bright red cheek. A real beauty about July 10th.

Louise—Medium; larger than Beatrice; excellent for home use; too tender for shipment. Ripens just after Beatrice.

Lady Farham—Large; green, with dull red cheek; very good. Last of October and first half of November.

Large September—Large, white, red blush. Reminds one of Old Mixon Free, but ripens in September. This is, no doubt, an old variety that has come to us without a name. Freestone.

Old Mixon Free—Large; white, with red cheek; juicy; excellent. July 10 to 15.

Old Mixon Cling—Large; white, mottled with red. An old peach of superior value. July 15th to 20th.

Picquet's Late—Large; yellow, red blush; flesh yellow; excellent. August 15th. Freestone.

Rivers—Large; pale straw color; very juicy; of the best quality; too tender for market; ripens just after Louise.

Tillotson—Medium; white, nearly covered with red; excellent; good market variety. June 10th. Freestone.

THE NORTHERN CHINESE race occupies the lower portion of the range belonging to the Persian race, and some varieties succeed below it. In our own region, on the line of 70, one or two varieties only are really valuable. This class produces such very large peaches that it is to be regretted that it does not occupy a wider belt of country.

NORTHERN CHINESE LIST OF PEACHES

Prices—30 cents each; $3.00 per dozen; $20.00 per hundred, except where otherwise stated.

Albert Sidney—Medium to large, oblong, yellowish white, with red cheek; flesh melting, and of the highest flavor. Middle of July.

Bernice—Large, yellow, mottled with dark crimson; flesh yellow, melting, juicy, excellent. Freestone. July 10th.

Chinese Cling—Very large and beautiful, but not as good quality as several of its seedling. July 15th. Useless in the coast range.

Carpenter's Cling—Large, white, sometimes marbled with carmine, sweet, juicy. Originated by Mr. Carpenter of Mountain City, Texas, July 15. This variety bears well about half of the time in the coast country, and is so fine that it ought to be planted here.

Gen. Lee—Above medium, oblong, creamy white with carmine wash; flesh finely grained, melting, very juicy and of high flavor; quality best. July 1st. Cling.

Juno—Very large, deep yellow, mottled orange crimson; flesh yellow, fine grained, excellent sub-acid. Clingstone. August 1st. The Bernice, Juno, Oriole, and Sylphide originated with Dr. L. E. Berkmans of Georgia.

Oriole—Large yellow, rich, buttery, excellent. Freestone. August 1st.

Spottswood—Similar to Chinese Cling. Very large, and of best quality. July 5th to 10th.

Sylphide—Similar to Chinese Cling, but a month later.

Stonewall—Almost similar to Gen. Lee, but about a week later, and tree a more upright grower. July 7th to 10th.

Thurber—Large to very large, skin white, with light crimson mottlings, juicy, delicate aroma, good enough for anybody. Originated by Dr. Berkmans, and first disseminated by P. J. Berkmans in 1873. Freestones bear in the coast country better than most of this class, but not here reliable in most places.

THE SPANISH RACE occupies, probably we may say, the entire range of the Northern Chinese race, and extends considerably Southword of it, the greater portion of the range of the *Southern* Chinese race being included in its proper habitation.

Prior to the introduction of the Chinese varieties, it seemed to be the only class of peaches that could be made a paying success here and below us. This race still comprises the bulk of the orchards in and near the isotherm of 70. It seems to do better a little above this line than below it. Its introduction into our horticulture was the really practical beginning of Southern Texas peach culture.

And now we think that in getting the new seedlings of Mr. Taber of Florida, we have additions to this list that will vastly increase its value.

SPANISH LIST OF PEACHES

Prices—40 cents each; $4 per dozen; $25 per 100; except where otherwise noted.

Bonito—Medium to large; yellow with beautiful carmine wash; flesh yellow with red near seed, very firm; takes a high color long before really ripe; stands shipment well; a very beautiful fruit, but not of first quality.

Cabler's Indian—Large, closely resembles Flewellen; purple, flesh containing deeper purple veins, sub-acid, decided Indian type, a good market peach. July 20th. Clingstone.

Countess—A new peach from Mr. G. L. Taber of Florida. Described by him as nearly round, large to very large; skin white; flesh white, tender, melting, juicy, vinous; quality excellent. Freestone. Will probably ripen here about July 5th to 10th. In *dormant bud this year 50 cents each*, after planting season of 1888-9 trees at 50 cents each.

Dowling's June—Another of Mr. Taber's seedlings. Medium to large, quite red, sub-acid. Clingstone. June.

Elma—One of Mr. Taber's peaches. Strongly resembling Old Mixon cling. Will probably ripen here about July 15th to 20th. Clingstone.

Galveston—Large, white, juicy, tender for shipment, but fills a place for those who prefer a white freestone for home use. July 25th to August 10th.

Guadalupe—Large, white sub-acid, good. August. Clingston.

Lula—Large, yellow; flesh yellow. About August 1. Freestone.

Lilard's October—Large, white, red cheek, fair flavor; bearing qualities not tested on the coast, will be likely to be found productive in this country. Obtained from Mr. Lilard at Seguin, Texas.

La Magnifique—Another of Mr. Taber's Florida seedlings. Tree strong grower, good bearer; fruit large, oblong; skin creamy white, washed with red; flesh firm, rich, sub-acid. Clingstone. Will probably ripen here about July 20th to August 1st. *Dormant buds 50 cents each*, for planting season of 1888-9; afterwards 50 cents per tree.

La Reine—A Florida seedling from Mr. Taber. Very large, slightly oblong; skin yellowish white, washed with red; flesh yellowish white, very red at the seed, firm, juicy, delicious. Will probably ripen here about July 10th to 15th. Clingstone. During the planting season of 1888-9, *50 cents each*; afterwards same as other varieties of this list.

Maggie Burt—Yellow clingstone with carmine cheek; a strong grower, good size. July 20th.

Onderdonk's Favorite—Large; skin and flesh yellow; very juicy and sweet; the best combination of quality, appearance and productiveness. Decidedly our favorite. July. Freestone. *Price, 50 cents each: $5 per dozen, when ordered alone.*

Orman—Large, round, yellow, with carmine wash. A rare beauty. Originated by Mr. Orman at Concrete, Dewitt county, Texas. September 1st. Clingstone.

Rose—Medium, round, rosy red, firm flesh, rich, juicy and sweet. June 25th. Freestone.

Rupley's Cling—Large, clear yellow, sometimes with a slight blush. The fruit was not large on our young trees, but as the trees attain age this variety excites the admiration of all who see it. July 20.

Sander's Cling—Large, bright yellow, very good. July 25th to August 1st.

Texas—Medium to large; dim green, shaded with red. Good freestone. Late in July.

Taber's No. 13—Very large; yellow washed with carmine. We will have it in dormant bud during the winter 1888-9, at *50 cents each*; afterwards trees at same rate as given at the head of this list. Clingstone.

Taber's No. 5—Resembles Lemon Cling and is therefore a showy peach. *50 cents each* in dormant bud during winter of 1888-9.

Victoria—Another of Taber's seedlings. Large, slightly oblong, creamy white, juicy, well flavored. About August 1st. Freestone. *50 cents* for dormant buds in winter of 1888-9.

THE SOUTHERN CHINESE RACE

Will probably be found successful in about all of the Southern third of the area properly covered by the Northern Chinese race, and extends a little below, or down to, the lower borders of the regions of the Spanish race. It is most valuable below the line of greatest success of the Spanish race. The breadth from North to South, of the proper home of this race will probably be found to be a narrow one. But on the isothermal line of 70 it is surely the most successful class of peaches known to horticulture.

Aside from the possibilities of obtaining a variety of the PEEN TO RACE that does not bloom too early on our line the Southern Chinese seems to be the material from which to expect to obtain our extra early varieties that are yet to be originated, to fill a place here similar to that occupied by the Alexander in the regions of success with the Persian race.

It is only about sixteen years since we began to become acquainted with this race of peaches. During this brief period its season of ripening has been extended in earlier and later varieties, about a month, and even this improvement has all been made within the last five years. If we shall meet with as good success during the years to come that we have had during the last half decade, then we shall yet, in one or more members of this race attain a degree of earliness never yet suggested by the wildest dreams.

There are now numerous choice varieties of this race. But our object is not to multiply varieties, but to secure a succession from the earliest varieties possible, to better fill the season between our earliest and the old varieties of July. Therefore, we present only the five varieties that we have selected as best suited to that object.

LIST OF SOUTHERN CHINESE PEACHES

Prices given relate to delivery at the Nursery.

Early China—Very clearly resembling Henry in fruit, but ripens seven to ten days earlier. The tree is of stronger growth and attains a greater size than Honey. Price, 75 cents each, $8 per dozen.

Honey—This peach was originated by Charles Downing, from seed obtained from China. The Original tree never fruited, but a budded tree was given to the late Henry Lyons, Esq., of Columbia, S. C., about 1855. The variety was placed in the hands of Mr. P. J. Berkmans, of Augusta, Ga., and the only stock held by him until 1858, when it was sent out for the first time. The variety was not found to be valuable at Augusta, but when it was sent to Florida and Texas, into its natural and proper home, it was found to possess special merit. We obtained our original stock from Mr. Berkmans. Medium, oblong, with sharp

HONEY PEACH.

recurved points, creamy white, washed with carmine; flesh of a peculiarly fine texture and a honey sweetness. June 5th to 20th. Price, 50 cents each, $5 per dozen.

Pallas—Originated by Mr. Berkman's. A seedling of the Honey. About same size as Honey or perhaps some larger, but more round in form. Flesh white, melting, with a rich vinous aroma, partaking in this the flavor of the Gross Mignonne. Ripens after Honey, but exact season not settled yet for this region as we have ripened it only twice. Price, 50 cents each.

Coleman—Originated by Thos. Coleman, near Rockport, Texas, and is given by him a description similar to that we have given of Pallas. Price, 50 cents in dormant bud during the winter of 1888-9, the same as Honey afterward.

Climax—Is larger than Honey; round, slightly oblong, with less recurved point that Honey; color pale yellow, washed with red; flesh yellowish white, fine grained, melting, sprightly, with a distinct trace of acid lacking in the Honey; quality good. Freestone. Ripens just after Honey. Price, 50 cents each; $5 per dozen.

THE PEEN TO RACE

Occupies the extreme Southern portion of the Southern Chinese range, and extends still below it, where no other peaches are known to exist. We do not doubt its capacity to thrive in a tropical climate, side by side with the banana, the pine apple, the cocoa nut, and citrous fruits of the tropics.

Writers have spoken of it as a "*strain*" of the Southern Chinese race. But the points of difference are so very striking, and its character so fixed as revealed by the character of its seedlings, that we believe it should not be denied the position given it by nature as a distinct *race*. While we do not like to multiply distinctions, yet we have always found it to be up-hill work to contend against the decisions of nature. While we have here, on the line of 70, produced some good crops of the Peen To, yet we have generally failed with it, and our hopes concerning its value for this region are relinquished, unless we can obtain a variety that blooms later than any Peen To that we have yet heard of.

There are Numerous seedlings of this class, but with the past history of our experience with the race in this region, we believe we are too much subject to polar influences to allow us to recommend the *Peen To* upon *our line*, and our trade far below us in the regions where it properly belongs is yet so light that we propagate but few trees of this class, and present only two varieties.

PEEN TO LIST OF PEACHES.

PEEN-TO.

Peen to—Resembles in form a large flat tomato, both ends being flattened, and the pit also partaking of the same form; greenish white, washed with carmine on the sunny side; when fully ripe is of a delicate waxen yellow; flesh pale yellow, sweet, juicy, and of fine flavor. Clingstone. Stone very small. Ripens here sometimes as early as May 25th. The fruit *here* has generally some bitterness near the skin which it does not possess in its proper home. This peach is a great favorite in Florida among the oranges. Price, 50 cents each, $5 per dozen.

Bidwell's Early—Originated in Florida by Mr. Bidwell of Orlando. Roundish oblong; size medium; skin creamy white, washed with carmine; flesh fine grained, juicy, sweet. Clingstone. Maturity about the same as Peen To.

PLUMS

No variety of European plums has succeeded in Southern Texas. Yet the Chickasaw and other Southern types have given us a good collection of choice varieties extending from the first of May to September. Some hybrids between the Chickasaw and European families have proven valuable in the Northern and interior portions of the State, but when brought to our coast region they have proven to be destitute of good bearing qualities. But when we attain a degree of hybridization in which the *Prunus Europea* is sufficiently dominant to overcome the disposition to sucker, and impart size and comeliness to the tree—and at the same time the *Prunus Chickasa* is sufficiently present to secure fruitfulness—*then* we have gained a point, in principle and in fact, for the plum culture of the extreme South that will prove truly a vast beginning. We believe that in the MARIANA, from Mr. Ely, we have a variety that attains to this combination. In our own grounds we have other varieties, of the same general origin, waiting more thorough tests before dissemination. Here is a new development in plum culture that promises vast results.

We have devoted a few acres to experiments with the plum. We have originated about four hundred varieties during our experience. The tests of time have established the value of several of these new varieties. Also, our collection has been enriched by valuable additions from other sources until we are willing to say that we have secured an excellent list of plums for the *extreme* South.

We shall continue to be extremely cautious about recommending varieties that will not merit public favor.

OUR LIST OF AMERICAN PLUMS.

(IN ORDER OF RIPENING.)

Price of Trees at the Nursery, 50 cents each, $4 per dozen. If delivered elsewhere we make a charge to cover cost and risk of shipment. Special rates for special selections and special sizes.

AFRICAN PLUM.

Early Red—Medium, round, pale carmine, usually ripens first week in May, sometimes in April. The earliest plum in our collection for Southern Texas. In Northern Texas Caddo Chief seems to precede it a little.

Caddo Chief—Medium, oblong, red. Ripens about four days after Early Red here. A surer bearer than Early Red, but not of as good quality.

Munson—A new variety from our own grounds and now offered for the first time. Large, oblong, vermillion red, as large as Wild Goose, and about two weeks earlier. Tree of low spreading habit, and a good bearer.

Jennie Lucas—Large, clear bright yellow, good flavor.

Piram—Large, round, pale green. Originated by P. T. Hall, formerly of Goliad County, Texas. A very heavy bearer.

Mariana—Large, round, red, sweet; bears mostly on old spurs. Tree a very fine grower, never suckers, makes a good shade tree, and should take the place of Umbrella China in many instances.

Coletta—Large, slightly oblong, pale carmine, sweet; a showy fruit. Tree has upright habit, is a heavy biennial bearer.

African—Large, round; russet with blush when ripening; dark flesh colored red when ripe; a sprightly sweet. About June 1st.

Wild Goose—Large, oblong, ripens from pale yellow to vermillion; ripens with African. About June 1st. There is much complaint in Southern Texas about its bearing habits. There are some trees in this region that bear enormously, and yet we have seen that the complaints against its bearing habits in this region generally are well founded.

Saffold—Large, round, red, decidedly acid; much valued for preserves. Tree a spreading open grower, bears well.

Clara—Somewhat larger than Saffold, of the same general character, but a trifle later. Named in honor of Miss Clara Davidson of Mission Valley, Texas, whose father has presented us with a seedling plum bearing a close resemblance to this variety.

Indian Chief—Large, round, red, sub-acid; flesh a little mealy; bears well at an extremely early age. Tree has an open habit, and, we think, is more subject to effects of extremes of wet and dry than most varieties. Very popular.

Beaty—Medium, round, red, sweet; very productive; ripens in succession, extending over more time than is usual with plums. Keeps remarkably well after gathering, and has the best possible shipping qualities.

Newman—An old variety of good standing. Medium, oblong, red, sweet, bear acquaintance well. July 20th to 25th here.

Kanawha—Medium, ripens from yellow to vermillion. August here. This variety, with the Golden Beauty, seems to belong to a new native type hitherto undescribed, but now being investigated by Prof. Munson.

Golden Beauty—We obtained this variety by cuttings from a wild tree near Fort Belnap at the close of the war between the states. We were so pleased with the appearance of the tree in full bearing that we named it *Golden Beauty*. Fruit yellow, quite handsome when thoroughly ripe, flesh firm, seed small, a choice variety for preserves. Ripens here August 15th to 25th.

ORIENTAL PLUMS

American pomology is being vastly enriched by introductions from the Orient. In plum culture, we of the extreme South have hitherto been confined to varieties of our own native races. But there has now come to us a hardy race from Japan, that seems destined to bear an important part in giving variety and enlargement to our supply of plums. The best tested of this group in the *Kelsey*. That it is productive both above and below our isothermal line and line of latitude is well determined. Then it remains to a certainty that it will prove successful here also.

The growth of the young trees here is all that could be desired. It is bearing well at Houston. At our nurseries we are having the first products this year. At this writing, July 6, we have just measured a specimen about six inches in circumference. It has probably yet six weeks to grow before maturity, so that it is easy to believe that it will reach a circumference of eight or nine inches.

To have a plum that can be readily peeled with a knife, as one would do a peach may seem extravagant, but it is just what we have in some of these Japan plums. We have eight varieties growing in our grounds at the nurseries. We shall be ready to supply any or all of them in the fall of 1889. We can supply them in dormant bud this season at 50 cents each, or $5 per dozen, on Mariana stocks.

Kelsey—Very large, sometimes reaching a circumference of nine inches. Dark brown yellow, with bush of pale red; sweet, flesh as firm as an apple; seeds not larger than we usually find in our small varieties. Season of maturity here about August 25th. Tree an upright grower, but does not probably attain a great size. 50 cents to $1, according to grade of tree.

Ogan—Botan—Chalot—Mason—Long-fruited—All are said to have the same general character as Kelsey, with variations of color and season.

Botankie—Is said to mature earlier, but we have not fruited it.

Virgata—Beautiful ornamental tree, blooming very early showing a profusion of rose colored double flowers. If the late frost does not prevent it bears a good crop of small, oblong, orange yellow plum of an apricot flavor.

Prunus Pissardii—This variety comes from Persia. The leaves are highly colored with a combination of purple and red, and maintain this color all through the season. This renders it a showy tree for the yard or garden. It fills the same place among flowering trees and shrubs as colored foliage plants do in the conservatory or flower garden. The fruit is large, bright red, fair quality, and ripens here this year in the second week of May. 50 cents to $1.

Prunus Simonii—A new fruit introduced from China. It is not known whether it will prove successful here. We have had it two years, 1887 and 1888 cover two years of our utmost extremes, and yet the trees seem to be doing well. We are trying it ourselves, and offer it to those who want to test its value here. Tree of medium height, upright habit, leaves deeply veined, but otherwise somewhat between those of peach and plum. The fruit is said to resemble a flattish, smooth, brick red tomato. The flesh has an apricot yellow color, firm, and with a peculiar aromatic flavor. It is like no other fruit with which we are acquainted. If it succeeds here it will probably mature here about last of June or first of July. 50 cents to $1 each.

~~~~~~~~~~~~~~~~

APPLES

A few years ago we had no faith in Apples for Western Texas; but we have watched eagerly every experiment bearing upon the question, until our sense of encouragement has ripened into a good degree of confidence. We find that in this region our young apple trees grow off with astonishing rapidity. After two or three years our standard trees assume a dwarf habit. They grow as large as a dwarf pear tree, and some varieties bear well. Out of about eighty varieties tested in our experimental orchards a few varieties have been found so far adapted as to be worthy of cultivation here. We raise altogether standard trees, as we find no artificial dwarfs to be valuable. As we ascend toward the interior, we find the apple does better than here. There is one general misapprehension about the apple which we wish to see corrected. It is often said that this country is "too dry" for the apple. Now, the apple and pear will bear more drought than the peach. I have not yet seen a season so dry as to seem to injure

my apple or pear trees, or injure the fruit. But apples must have good soil and good cultivation.

LIST OF APPLES

Prices of trees, 40 cents each; $4.00 per dozen; $20.00 per 100.

Red May—Medium, nearly covered with red; ripens with us about last of May and early in June.

Harvest—Medium, yellow; follows Red May in time of ripening.

Summer Queen—Large, yellow, with rich strips of carmine; ripens in June.

Stevens—Medium to small, flat, well covered with red; flavor good; originated with Mr. Stevens at Gonzales. Ripens with Summer Queen.

Yellow Sweet—Large, yellow; a good bearer and the only sweet apple that has done well enough to seem valuable to our culture; follows Stevens and Summer Queen.

Red Astrachan—Large, Red; is less reliable here than the other varieties; a fine apple; tree bears young; ripens in June.

Jones' Favorite—A straggling grower, but good bearer; medium to large, oblong, green, good flavor; ripens in August.

Lincoln—Large, flatish; while growing resembles Rhode Island Greening, but takes a dull blush just before ripening. Our best apple, August.

Sally Gray—Medium size; red on one side; flat, juicy, subacid; tree vigorous but does not bear as young as the other varieties. August and September.

Lincoln's Wonder

Ben Davis—A large, handsome, striped apple of fine quality. Tree very vigorous and productive; a fine keeper, highly esteemed but not well tested here; bears well 100 miles above us.

Shockly—A late variety, generally considered valuable at the South; fruit medium to small, roundish, conical, pale yellow; keeps remarkably well. We *hope* we have a good thing in the Shockly, but *do not know it*.

Transcendent Crab—Valued altogether for preserving.

PEARS

Our experience and observations concerning the pear have convinced us that if the proper varieties are selected it is well worth our care and attention to plant pear trees.

We have planted in orchard rows about seventy varieties and awaited results. At the end of fifteen years we have settled upon a few varieties that seem adapted to our soils and climate. Altogether our close study of the pear for Southern Texas extends over only a period of about twenty years. At first we had no faith in pear culture for our section. But after our results we should be dull indeed if we did not believe in planting pear trees on every premises that has a suitable situation.

At first we were impressed with an idea that dwarf pear trees would prove most promising. But our experience has reversed our judgment. We now declare decidedly in favor of *Standard* trees as a final dependence for fruit. However, we favor the planting of dwarfs for a quick supply till the standards can have time to come to bearing.

We supply both standard and dwarf trees. Dwarf trees are simply those raised on quince stocks. They bear soon and die early.

Standard trees are raised upon pear roots. They root very deep, defying the dryest season when once established. Both standard and dwarf bear drought well. Both insist upon clay at some accessible depth. The roots of the standard will run down to a great depth, reaching to a distance of thirty feet or more in good clay.

We would plant standards twenty feet each way, and then plant dwarfs between each two standards, so that every other row would all be dwarf and the remaining ones half standard and half of them dwarf trees. Our preference for standard trees is gaining ground every year.

Dwarf trees may be planted so that the joint with the quince will be from three to six inches below the surface of the ground. They will start more slowly, but will finally become half standard, and consequently longer lived. Standard trees should be planted at the same depth they stood in the nursery. Pear trees must be expected to grow off slowly at first for two or three years. Dwarf and standard trees will be sold at the same price.

No section has a long list of really successful pears. While the entire list of pears in cultivation embraces some fifteen hundred or more varieties, yet only a very few sorts succeed thoroughly in any one region. We have reduced our list to such as seem most promising here. We have not yet seen a case of pear blight in Southern Texas.

Price of Trees—50 cents each; $5.00 per dozen at the nurseries, except where otherwise stated. If delivered elsewhere we make a charge to cover cost and risk of delivery. *Special assortments and special sizes special rates.*

LIST OF PEARS

Andrews—Slow grower, scrubby habit, but finally bears well. Medium size, very rich; succeeds both as dwarf and standard. One of our good pears. July 20th.

Beurre Bosc—Long, fleshy stem, good quality; one of our best bearers. July

Belle Lucrative—Large, delicious; comes slowly into bearing; best as standard.

Bartlett—Large, rich; popular everywhere; very good here as a dwarf—better as a standard. August.

Duchesse c'Angouleme—Our largest good pear, excellent quality; bears well here; best as dwarf.

Kieffer—A seedling of the Chinese sand pear. A very strong grower; very promising but not thoroughly tested here.

Le Conte—A seedling of the Chinese sand. The most vigorous grower we have seen. Its bearing habits exceed any other variety. Our oldest Le Conte tree is now a sight worth taking pains to see. It was planted eight years ago and has now an astonishing crop. But we think it must be conceded that the Le Conte is a sand pear, as it seems to do very much the best in a sandy soil. From what we have seen of this variety we intend to increase our planting in orchard rows. In quality Le Conte is about as good as the Bartlett is here, conceding that *our* Bartletts are not as good as at the North.

QUINCES.

When properly treated the quince does well here. Nothing turns up its nose quicker at a poor soil than the quince. Plant in rich soil, apply a little salt on the surface of the ground each year. The Apple or Orange quince is well tested here. Price 50 cents.

FLEMISH BEAUTY.

MULBERRIES.

Texas is a part of the natural home of the Mulberry. We can scarcely mention a variety of soil in which the Mulberry, in its numerous varieties, does not thrive well. While our native wild varieties are of good quality, yet they ripen through such a very brief season that it is welcome to have varieties that continue through a longer period. We believe we are on the eve of marked improvements in the Mulberry. The introduction of the Russian type is a matter of importance to the American people. Although it is true that in planting what nurserymen now offer as simply "*Russian Mulberry*" trees, the purchaser cannot have any possible intimation whether the fruit on his trees will be white, black or red; large, small or medium, because they are all seedlings, yet he *may* know that he is getting something that will grow rapidly, and if properly pruned up will make a fine thrifty tree. It remains to develop from this hardy race a list of valuable varieties of special merit. We are trying to see what we can do towards developing good varieties from the Russian type, and we expect in time to present a good collection.

We are led to believe that in situations where they can be cultivated for three or four years after planting, the seedling Russian Mulberry is a valuable tree to plant to serve as posts to a wire fence. It has the merit of standing almost any wind that ever blows. During the cyclone of 1886 not one of our Russian Mulberry trees were injured. We have trees planted four years ago that were large enough a year ago to serve as posts to a wire fence. We do not know how durable the timber would prove when set in the ground as post. Our proposition is to use the growing tree as it stands.

LIST OF MULBERRIES.

English—We find this variety here, pleasing everybody who has it. We do not know whether this is its proper name. We doubt it. But it is the name by which our people know it. Tree a round spreading head, makes a fair shade tree. Berries large, long, acid, continues ripening for several weeks, and sometimes also makes a Fall crop. 50 cents each, $5 per dozen.

Rives—A very fine rapid growing *shade tree*. The fruit, while being good, has not special merit. The value of this variety consists in its capacity to make a good shade *quickly*. 50 cents to $1, according to size.

Russian Mulberry—All seedlings, and may produce fruit of any color or size, or none at all. A quick growing Ornamental Tree. 25 to 50 cents, according to size; $5 to $10 per 100, according to size.

Emma—A new seedling, originated upon our premises, and seems to be a cross between the wild mulberry and one of our cultivated sorts. Tree a strong grower, leaves very large; berry large, sub-acid, has an extended season of ripening. $1.

Victoria—One of our new varieties developed from the Russian type. A tall upright grower, very rapid growth, a great favorite on our premises. Berry large, sweet, black, ripens for several weeks. $1 each, $8 per dozen.

GRAPES

Many of our people have planted grapes and have failed. Some have deserved and experienced failures, because they have not taken care of their vines. But others have *failed because they planted varieties not suited to the climate*. We have spared neither attention nor expense to make our experience with Grapes as valuable as possible. We have been cultivating the Grape for thirty years on our present premises. We are pleased with the progress that we have made in ascertaining the adaptability of varieties to our climate. As it takes several years to properly test some varieties, we must expect slow progress in this kind of enterprise. Our experience has led us to adopt some generalization which seem to be correct and are of vast service in selecting for experiment.

117

Some years ago we planted sixty varieties of grapes in our experimental vineyard. Our collection embraced varieties belonging to every family of grapes then considered worthy of cultivation. The only thoroughly successful varieties in our experiments belong to what was then spoken of as the *Southern Æstivalis* type.

We had temporary success with some Labruscas and some Vinifera varieties. But, from different causes, we found them unreliable and short lived with us. Further towards the interior, and in special localities where conditions are different from our own, some varieties that failed with us have given good results. But we believe that our results hold as a general guide for the coast region, that they are a less certain guide as we recede from the coast country and gain higher latitudes, greater elevations, and attain different conditions.

Prof. T. V. Munson of Dennison, Texas, is doing valuable service for the future viticulture of Texas. He has many new seedlings which, altogether, include quite every combination from which we hope to secure new varieties with which to improve our collections for *Southern* as well as Northern Texas. Several of these new grapes are now in our experimental vineyard awaiting the test of time before being offered to the public. We may well hope that Mr. Munson's labors will yet enable all Southern Nurserymen to enlarge their list of profitable grapes.

PLANTING THE VINES.

We refer the reader to our chapter on Selection of ground for orchards. He should remember that drainage is above every other consideration. Prepare the ground as thoroughly as for any other crop. Our Southern varieties should be planted not closer than ten or twelve feet apart each way. To prepare the plant shorten the roots to six or eight inches. We cut the tops to within a foot or less of the old wood of the plant.

If the soil is rich enough to produce twenty or twenty-five bushels of corn to the acre it is rich enough for starting a vineyard. *Put no fresh manure* in the neighborhood of the roots. There may be situations having no clay sub-soil in which extra deep holes or deep trenches are an advantage, but deep trenching or deep holes into the clay subsoil has proven, with us, worse than labor thrown away. Many a tree and vine has been killed by this sort of kindness. The hole may be made from nine to eleven inches deep, and then filled to within about from six to eight inches with good moist surface soil. It is best to plant while the earth from the hole is moist and fresh.

Insert the plant so that only one or two buds may be above the surface at the completion of the planting. If, when the plant is held as above directed, it is thereby brought to a leaning position, no harm, but rather advantage will result. Now cover the roots with moist surface soil, and press it well around the roots. Should the soil not be well moist pour some water into the hole before packing the earth. Let is soak away and complete the filling as in other planting.*

The above method of planting secures more or less eyes before the surface of the ground. These will each send out a number of roots, greatly reinforcing those with which the vine is planted, and thus securing a much stronger growth than could be obtained by planting none of the wood of the top.

PRUNING THE GRAPE.

Universal experience teaches that the best results are obtained from the new sprouts which grow from the *strongest shoots of the previous year's growth*. Any system of pruning therefore, to be correct, must encourage a good annual supply of such growth. In this climate, also, every cluster of grapes must be *in the shade*. Aside from the above essentials any peculiarities of any system are mere matters of taste or convenience. We give only one system and refer the reader who wishes to study other methods, as well as gain a large fund of useful information—to Prof. Geo. Husmann's new work, entitled "American Grape Growing and Wine Making," sold by Orange Judd & Co., New York. Also, *Illustrated American Grapes*, by Bush and Son and Meissner, Bushberg, Mo.

* See under How to Plant a Tree, page 4.

119

Grapes on Vine One Year Old, Root Planted in March, 1908. Photo October 25th Following. Farm of H. G. Stillwell, San Benito, Texas

During the first Summer let the plants grow just as they please—stakes or trellis not being required.

During the Winter after the first year of growth cut away all of the previous year's growth except three eyes. Before the vines start their spring growth the soil should be well cultivated, the plants hoed clean and stakes set along each row to support the wires of the trellis. The lower wire will only be needed during this season and may be placed about eighteen inches from the ground.

During the Spring of the second year a number of shoots will start from the stump of three eyes which was left at the winter pruning. When these shoots are about six or eight inches long, the first summer pruning begins by removing all of these shoots except two. These two shoots should be trained to the wire, which is about eighteen inches quite immediately above them, if it has been properly arranged. These shoots, while young, will be found very tender, and care will be needed not to injure them in handling. We sometimes use light switches set in the ground as supports, tying the tender shoots to them till they reach the wire. We prefer strings made by stripping up the leaves of the Spanish Dagger tree, or *Yucca Gloriosa*, as they will rot off just about the right time. Train these two shoots along the wire in opposite direction. Allow no new shoots from below. Remove all the side shoots from these two main canes for from four to six feet from their base, but do not injure the buds in so doing. Keep the soil well cultivated all summer. These two canes which we call horizontal arms, should each grow to from fifteen to thirty feet during the year, and we have seen them make forty-five feet.

During the Winter after the second year of growth, cut the horizontal arms back to from four to six feet each—the length of the shortened cane to be governed by the growth of the former year. *Always cultivate the soil and hoe the plants before the new growth appears and continue* thorough cultivation through the season. Now add the two remaining wires to complete the trellis. The lower wire having ten to twelve inches from the first. The third or upper wire may be eighteen or twenty inches above the middle one, so that the trellis would consist of three wires, the highest being about four feet from the ground. Some cultivators use four wires, No. 12 wire is the size generally preferred.

During the Spring after the second pruning, which is the third year after planting, we find the plant consisting of two horizontal arms, from four to six or possibly eight feet long—everything else having been cut away. The cultivator may now expect a reasonable crop of grapes. Bind these two arms to the lower wire of the trellis. This should be done before the Spring growth has begun. A sprout will start from each bud of the horizontal arms. Select on the upper side of the arms from five to seven of the strongest bearing shoots and train them as upright canes, binding them to the second wire. Rub off all shoots except those selected as upright canes. If any appear feeble remove the weaker ones. If any buds have made two shoots remove the weakest one. If some are not yet developed, we pass them for the present and go over the vines again in four or five days afterwards. All of the fruit is to be grown on these new shoots. In our treatment of the grape we simply train these shoots to the wires above them and along on the trellis, as this answers the purposes for which we cultivate the vine, and it will be found by most cultivators to best suit their convenience. But for those who desire to make the very largest and finest clusters, and are willing to tax themselves with the additional labor and care to insure that object, we recommend the renewal system.

Summer Pruning.—Near the base of each of the horizontal arms, select a strong shoot, which is to be trained for the purpose of *renewal* at the next winter pruning. This renewal cane, as it grows is to be trained to the upper wire of the trellis.

Next pass over the remaining upright canes and pinch off the terminal bud of each as soon as it reaches two leaves beyond the last bunch of grapes, the embryo clusters of which will appear as the cane grows. Some varieties will show two, others three, and the Herbemont and Lenoir will sometimes show four bunches of fruit on one of these upright canes.

After the upright canes have been stopped as above directed, they will start lateral from the axis of each leaf. The laterals should be promptly stopped by pinching each one off just above the first leaf. The sooner this is done after the lateral passes the development of its first leaf the better. In fact, every operation of Summer pruning should be performed *as soon as the development of the plant will admit.*

The laterals will start a second time, when we in turn pinch off this new growth to one leaf as before, thus giving to each lateral two leaves. The above stopping of canes and laterals will force a development of fruit by stopping all surplus growth and at the same time supply abundant shade for the growing grapes. The whole course of pruning will here, with our Southern varieties, be completed by the middle of April or a very little later, and whatever grows afterwards during the season may be left to grow at will on the trellis, except that suckers from near the ground must be kept down during the whole season.

During the Winter after the third year of growth we do our third Winter pruning. Of course, we must now be governed by the conditions resulting from the Summer treatment of the preceding year of growth. If we followed the renewal system of Summer pruning we will now see that each vine consists of the two horizontal arms which support the upright fruit canes of the previous year, and the *renewal* canes which we trained to the upper wire of the trellis. There may also be more or less light, straggling shoots that may have escaped amputation, so that the vine shall again consist of only two horizontal arms, trained in opposite direction on the lower wire of the trellis.

But if we have not followed the *renewal system* of summer pruning, our vines will be in a different form and will, of course, require different treatment. In the latter case instead of two strong canes on the upper wire and several short old fruit arms, we will find several upright canes of considerable strength. If we see that one of these canes has very much outgrown all the rest and it comes from near the base of the plant, we cut away all the rest on that side, and make a *renewal* cane of it as in the pruning after the renewal system. But if the canes are of something like equal growth (as they will usually be found to be), then we cut each one back to within four eyes of the old wood. If a cane appears much stronger than the average it might have an eye or two more; or if below an average it may be left with an eye or two less. And if there are a good number of strong canes, say five to seven on a side, then any very *weak* ones could be cut out altogether or at most given a single eye.

From this onward the treatment of each succeeding year is to be a repetition of this year's work. By this time the cultivator will have become acquainted with his vines, and will have acquired sufficient judgment concerning them that he should be competent to manage them successfully.

There are some points in relation to the treatment of the grape to which we will here refer at the risk of some repetition. Whatever system of pruning is adopted the work must be begun *early and pressed promptly,* so rapid is the Spring development that delay is disastrous. Do all stopping of shoots so early that it can be done at the terminals, so that the vine shall be despoiled of little or no foliage, and there shall be no waste by forming useless wood, only to be removed during the growing season. The grape is very sensitive to the loss of foliage during the season of rapid growth—therefore the idea in summer pruning is *not to destroy foliage or new wood, but to so direct their formation as to economize every energy of the plant and concentrate its power to the production of fruit.* The operator who fails to keep these ends in view had better not summer prune at all.

Again, it must be remembered—and the idea carried through our pruning and binding to the trellis—that while young fruit may grow well in the sun, yet in this latitude the *grapes must be in the shade at the ripening season.*

Again, *don't cut your vines while the buds are swelling,* as it will cause them to bleed so freely. If you have begun to cut and find them bleeding very much, then wait till a norther has checked the sap and begin to open, and although we deprecate cutting at this stage, yet it is better than to prune when the vines bleed profusely. And yet again, don't cut too early, as then the warm spells of our winter may push out the fruit buds too soon and thus endanger the crop. The middle of our January is the safest medium time for our winter pruning.

OUR LIST OF GRAPES.

We have thrown aside the largest number of varieties which we have been cultivating, because we have not found them adapted to this region. Although many catalogues contain long lists of grapes, yet the list of really profitable varieties in every locality is very short. Large amounts of money are annually squandered in the vain hope of success with a large number of varieties. This is a delusion against which we wish to caution our people. As a large portion of Texas is infested by phylloxera we have taken care that our list should be mostly composed of varieties found to be phylloxera proof. We will supply any variety, whether in our list or not, if *early* application is made.

We are satisfied that the classification of grapes is about to undergo a general revolution, and we shall, therefore, in our descriptions, avoid such descriptive terms as we think will soon become obsolete, and use only such as will remain intelligible.

We shall hasten to add to our list any new varieties that are ready for dissemination, as soon as we have sufficient reason to believe that they will be valuable to our people.

Price of Plants at Nursery—25 cents each; $2.50 per dozen; $10.00 per 100, *except in cases where other rates are appended.* Wholesale rates given on application. Special assortments at special rates. *These prices apply in cases only in which delivery is made at the nursery.* If delivered elsewhere we make an additional charge to cover cost of transportation and risk in transit.

LIST.

Black July (Herbemont type)—Medium, black, sweet, seldom shouldered, compact; ripens early in July. We think it a little too far South in the coast region; an excellent table grape. It is a pity that it bears so lightly and fails so young here. It is durable and productive further up the country, nearer the climate of its origin. This variety has been found wild in different places in Georgia and Alabama. It is also known as Deveraux, Sumpter, Lincoln, Sherry, Blue Grape, and at one time was disseminated as Lenoir.

Harwood (Herbemont type)—We obtained this grape from Major Harwood of Gonzales. It seems to have come as a sport from the Herbemont in his garden. The original plant was very productive and vigorous. It does not start well from cuttings, and is generally raised by grafting. It seems to be somewhat eccentric in habit. In some situations it is simply splendid, in others a flat failure. It seems to do best on mustang stocks. This variety will never become cheap on account of the mode required for propagation. 50 cents each; $5.00 per dozen.

Louisiana (Herbemont type)—Bunch and berry medium; compact, sweet, gray-purple. Middle of July.

Herbemont—Often known as Warren. Berry medium, dark purple, blue bloom, cluster large, heavily shouldered, compact, very thrifty and productive. Our strongest grower, our best wine grape that has been thoroughly tested, and a good table grape. July 12th to 25th.

Cunningham (Herbemont type)—Bunch small, berry medium; amber or pale red, and, like all of Herbemont type, has little pulp.

Lenoir (Herbemont type)—Berry medium, black, round, no pulp, vinous and *very much coloring matter*; bunch large, long, compact, generally shouldered; leaves deeply lobed. This variety does not bear quite as young as the Herbemont. It is cultivated in different parts of the state under the names of *Black Spanish, El Paso, Burgundy* and *Jacques*. It has also been confounded with the Ohio or Cigar Box; but having obtained from Mr. Campbell a plant of the latter, we can testify that these varieties are very distinct. In France it is cultivated under the name of Jacques. It is there much demanded both on account of the very deep color of its wine and its capacity to resist the phylloxera, which are so rapidly destroying the vineyards of that country—and with others of its class will be useful in reconstructing the vineyards of California. The Lenoir and Herbemont are, without doubt, the two best vineyard grapes for Southern Texas that have yet come largely into cultivation.

Medora—A new seedling from Lenoir crossed by us upon Croton. We have long been trying to procure a variety of the Herbemont type that should fill the want of this section for a phylloxera-proof *white* grape. We think we have it in the Medora. We now offer it to the public for the first time. Time must prove whether this grape will please our people. Berry medium, cluster small-shouldered; white with white bloom; sometimes shows veins of purple on sunny side; very sweet. Foliage resembles Lenoir. We gave the seed producing this grape to Dr. Thos. Cocke of Victoria, Texas, who brought the vine to bearing. We named the variety after his daughter, now Mrs. Taylor of this county. Should the Medora not fill the position for which it has been originated we hope for an equivalent from among the white varieties of the same type originated by Prof. Munson. Price $1.00, mailed to any address or delivered at nursery.

Sweet Water (*of the European type V. Vinifera*)—Large, round, sweet, fleshy pulp, large clusters; has long been cultivated in Southern Texas as *Malaga*. A very fine table grape. Its value for us is much impaired by the fact that the vine, like all of its class, is subject to be destroyed by phylloxera, and therefore it is very short lived in Southern Texas generally. At points where phylloxera has not yet infested the grape it is a very vigorous grower. In the loose sands of the coast where it is presumed phylloxera cannot work this variety will probably always be in demand. But at such points as Galveston where other soils have been introduced in filling low sites, these varieties will probably uniformly fail. This variety is also subject to rot badly in unfavorable seasons. But it is so good when you *do* succeed with it that it is still demanded by our customers. We understand it to be a seedling of Malaga.

Malaga (*V. Vinifera*)—We got our start of true Malaga from California. The vines come into first bearing here this year. The fruit is lost by rot during this very rainy season. Berry large, pear-shaped, sweet, white, bunches very large; a splendid table grape. We don't claim to know how it will finally turn out here. We are *trying it* and offer it to others who want to see what they can do with it.

~~~~~~~~~~~~~~~~~~~~~

MISCELLANEOUS FRUITS.

Prices given are for trees at the nursery.

Almonds—The Peach Almond is hardy and productive here. It is, however, an inferior variety. Of the fine varieties, the *Princess* is the most promising. While the almond will likely prove of value in the higher portions of the state, yet the best varieties have not been successful with us. Price of trees 50 cents each; $5.00 per dozen.

Raspberries have promised just enough to induce perseverance with them, but never really successful. We have abandoned their culture.

Blackberries—We have repeatedly tried the fine varieties cultivated at the North and East. They have flattered us for a couple of years and then failed. We have finally tried a variety originating on the premises of Mr. Braden in Colorado County, Texas. It seems to be a cross between the wild Blackberry of Eastern Texas and the Texas Dewberry. It is doing so well with us that we are pleased with it and are disseminating it among our customers. We call it *Braden's Blackberry*. Price, $3 per dozen; $20 per 100.

Brunswick Figs.

Dewberries—Texas is the most natural home of the Dewberry. We consider them better than any Blackberry we ever knew. We have both *white* and black varieties. Price, $3 per dozen; $10 per 100.

Currants and Gooseberries with us have never survived the first season.

Cherries—We have tried many varieties of cherries. We have totally failed. We have no cherry trees for sale, but if ordered from us early will get them from the best Southern sources for our customers. 50 cents each; $5 per dozen.

Jujube—A fruit somewhat between a plum and a date. Foliage ornamental, hardy and vigorous here—*suckers badly.* We plant it for ornament and for our bees. 50 cents each; $4 per dozen.

Pomegranates—Sweet and sour. 40 cents each.

Japan Persimmon—We planted trees of this fruit in 1878. They are thrifty and productive. We believe this fruit will prove an acquisition to Southern Texas. The fruit of our trees have all been seedless. Some samples measured nine inches in circumference. While the trees do well, yet there are obstacles to the propagation of young trees here that will keep the price unreasonably high for some time. Present price of trees, $1 each.

ORNAMENTAL DEPARTMENT.

In the Pomological Department of Horticulture we have been compelled to advance step by step, by the accumulating light of experience and observation in a country where we had but few precedents to guide us. In the Ornamental Department we have had to contend with obstacles less formidable. But careful experiments and active observation enable us to glean here and there a gem. The love of flowers has induced many of our people to plant their favorites about their homes. Numberless experiments are thus made in this interesting field by those

Bananas. Bulbs Planted in January. Photo October 25th following. Farm of H. G. Stilwell, San Benito, Texas.

131

who have no public object in view; but they, nevertheless, unconsciously aid in the improvement of Texas floriculture. In our study we have combined these developments with our own experience to no small advantage. We do not claim that everything possible has been done in the Ornamental Department of Texas Horticulture, but we are highly encouraged by the collective results that have been attained. When we think of the grand army of experimenters in Texas, some of whom have public, and many of whom have only private objects in view; and when we consider the richness and value of our Southern floral wealth, we are led to look for a vast degree of development in the future. We are fast learning what trees, plants and flowers are suited to our region. We at first gave our whole attention to the subject of fruit culture. More recently we have been among the flowers. We well know that we have much to do to place this department of our establishment where it will meet the future demands of our patrons. But we shall spare no effort of which we are capable to keep pace with the increasing wants of our people.

We annually improve and extend our ornamental lists by importations. When, from year to year, we bring out new plants, we can easily bring as many more as are required by our customers. We will, therefore, accept orders for *anything desired* by our patrons that our list does not contain, provided, that such orders are forwarded in time to enable us to include them in our own importations, which will be made in November.

DECIDUOUS TREES, SHRUBS AND VINES.

We have rejected from our list all such as have been found unsuited to our climate. Many trees and shrubs of decided value at the North are often called for and *not supplied* because if our customers *must* fail with them we prefer to have them fail with stock from *some other nursery.*

DECIDUOUS LIST.

Prices all relate to delivery at the nursery. If delivered elsewhere we charge sufficient to cover cost and risk of transportation.

Althea (Rose of Sharon)—Shrub attaining 6 to 8 feet. Bears large flowers, continuing to bloom from May to October: double white, pink, purple, variegated. We have no single variety. 40 cents.

Box Elder—A rapid growing, native shade tree; attains the height of from 20 to 30 feet. 50 cents.

Crape Myrtle (*Lagerstræmia*)—Shrub attaining here 10 to 15 feet, perhaps should be called a tree. Bears exceedingly delicately fringed flowers in great profusion from May to October; hardy here; pink, purple and scarlet. 40 cents.

Crape Myrtle—White; of same family as above, not quite so hardy, more dwarf in habit, an abundant bloomer all summer; pure white. 50 cents.

Catalpa—Western Catalpa. 50 cents.

Chinese Evergreen (Hollii)—and Belgian (Lonicera Belgica) 40 Cents.

Flowering Pomegranate—Blooms freely in Spring; double flowers; two varieties, variegated and scarlet. 50 cents.

Flowering Willow (Chilopsis)—Purple. Native of West Texas; bears a profusion of bell shaped purple flowers; curious and beautiful; blooms from March to October.

Flowering Willow, white—A new variety, now for the first time introduced to the public. It was found by Dr. Atlee of Laredo, Texas in the sand of the Rio Grande near the seminary at Laredo. We obtained it from him, and now have a few plants for sale. It will be considered very beautiful by all who see it. The foliage is of a paler green than the purple which we began to disseminate when we first started our nursery in 1870. Price of plants, $1 each.

Honeysuckle (Lonicera)—Red Trumpet.

Japan Quince (Pyrus Japonica)—Bears red flowers early in the Spring. 50 cents.

Japan Quince (Pyrus Manlei)—Blooms freely in the Spring, blooms not so bright as the above, but produces considerable crops of fruit. 50 cents.

Lombardy Poplar—A tall, fine growing habit, much fancied by some; a good tree for quick effect, but is short lived here. 50 cents.

Locust (Black Locust)—Too well known to need description. 50 cents for single trees; $4 per dozen.

Maple (Silver Leaved)—Does well with us as long as we cultivate the soil. Succeeds in moist situations without special care, but fails in dry situations if not cared for. 50 cents each; $4 per dozen.

Silver Leaf Poplar—Leaves a bluish green on the upper side, a clear dazzling white on the under side of the leaves. When the leaves are stirred by the breeze the tree presents the appearance of being full of large white flowers. Sprouts from the roots and therefore requires to be kept succored. 50 cents.

Smoke Tree (Rhus Cotinus)—A shrub. Bears a fringe of hair like-flowers of smoky color; blooms at intervals all Summer. 50 cents.

Spirea Prunifolia—A low shrub, blooms very freely, bearing a great profusion of small, compact, double white flowers not larger than a shirt button. These grow all along the slender canes of the shrub. It is called Bridal Wreath by many persons. The blooms come about the time of Pyrus Japonica when flowers are scarce and help the appearance of a plot at that season. Later in the season they cease blooming and become inconspicuous. 40 cents.

Spirea Reevesii—This Spirea blooms a trifle later than Prunifolia; bears immense clusters of white open flowers (is also called Bridal Wreath by many) is very sightly during its brief season of blooming and has the merit of being *inconspicuous* after the blooming is over. Every ornamental plot should contain some of this *best of Spireas*. 40 cents.

Umbrella China—Too well known to require description; our most rapid growing shade tree. If customers at a distance order large trees they will not come above quotations given, unless extra sizes are called for, but it must be remembered that large trees of China have enormous roots and will necessitate high expressage. 25 to 50 cents.

Wistaria—Vigorous runner, bears spikes of light blue in early Spring. 50 cents.

EVERGREEN TREES AND SHRUBS.

Arbor Vitæ, Golden—Grows very compact and symmetrical without shearing; takes a yellow tint in Winter; makes a beautiful tree in the yard, or for a country lot. $1 for one foot, larger trees in proportion.

Arbor Vitæ, Intermedia—A cross between the common Chinese and golden, being less open than Chinese, and less compact than Golden; suits the fancy of some better than either of its parents. $1 for 1 to 2 feet; larger trees in proportion.

Arbor Vitæ, Globosa—A close growing tree often sold by some dealers as Golden. The foliage is of a darker green than Golden and serves a purpose of variety where Golden are also planted. One foot, $1; 2 feet, $2; 3 feet $3 each.

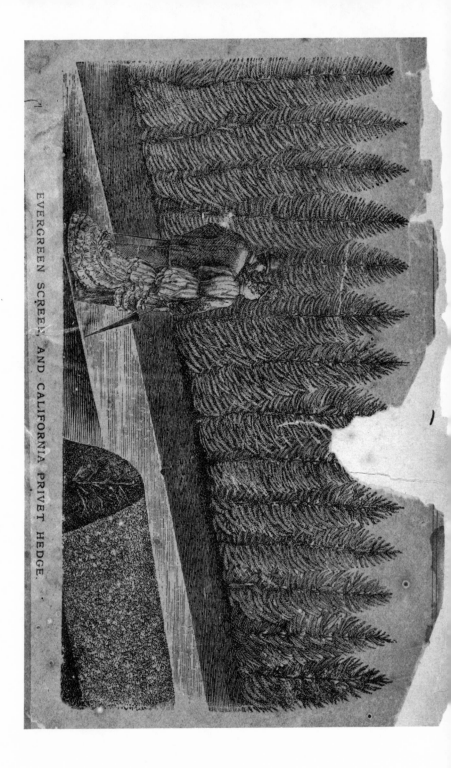

EVERGREEN SCREEN, AND CALIFORNIA PRIVET HEDGE.

Arbor Vitæ, Pyramidal—An upright grower of open habit while small. Naturally takes a pyramidal form, but if sheared to a pillar makes a good looking shaft-like evergreen; not subject to the diseases of the Pyramidal Cypress which we have tried to use for that purpose. $1 to $3.

Cypress—We have been experimenting with many varieties of oriental evergreen Cypresses. We thought we had several that we could recommend for this country. We have trees thirty feet high of one or two varieties and we had many lovely specimens embracing fifteen varieties in our grounds. We *thought* we had found a class of evergreen trees that was of value to our people. But the diseases that have stolen in upon them, and the severe tests of extremes in our climate during the last three years have reversed our estimate of the value of this family of evergreens for Southern Texas. We have found that among the *Biotas* (Arbor Vitæ) and *Cedars* we have material with which to obtain quite all of the effects in landscape work for which we had depended upon the Cypress family. We have, therefore, banished from our lists the Cypresses in all of its varieties, and increased our list of Biota and largely increased our culture of the Virginia Cedar.

Red Cedar—We cultivate largely the Virginia Cedar so common east of the Mississippi river. Our trees, being all seedlings, present a great number of varieties each having its peculiar style of form, foliage and general habit, so that we can select cedars bearing almost any required character. Our cedars are all *nursery raised* and have been root pruned four times so that they stand removal well. One foot, 50 cents; eighteen inches, 75 cents; 2 to 3 feet, $1.00. Larger trees supplied at special rates for special sizes.

Red Cedar Sheared—We have on hand *sheared* cedars so trained that the purchaser can develop any form desired. We

HORIZONTAL CYPRESS.

138

sometimes have them imitate the form of the Golden Arbor Vitæ, thus securing another shade of green to give variety to grounds having other low growths. $1 to $3.

Retinospora—We have tried every variety of this family that we could hear of. We have failed with all except one. This one comes without a name. We have sent samples to several specialists in order to determine its identity. No two have agreed about it. But it seems to do so well here that we do not propose to throw it aside for want of a name. So not knowing what it should be called and yet being compelled to designate it in some convenient way we shall call it Texas Retinospora until we can know its true name. It has a beautiful healthy-leaved foliage much resembling that of Thunga Ericoides; grows compactly; and ashy green; attains the height of six feet. $1.

Ceniza (*Leucophyllum Texana*)—We have never known of this shrub being given a place in any catalogue. And yet few are better entitled to admittance. We think that it ought to be in every family ground of the extreme South, and as far North as it is capable of existing. We at first thought it would only thrive in barren calcareous soils like those in which we find it in nature, but having tested it in various soils we are prepared to say that it will grow in any well drained soil.

A broad leaved evergreen having small oval leaves of ashy color. This color gives the Spanish name to the plant Ceniza being the Spanish word for ashes, The leaves have a pungent flavor and are of medical value. When smoked as tobacco they give a singularly soothing effect upon the respiratory organs, often relieving a cough. An infusion of the leaves is employed by the Mexicans and residents of Southwest Texas as a stomachic. It is also chewed in order to tighten loose teeth.

At frequent intervals it produces large crops of purple flowers. It makes a very pretty shrub for an ornamental plot, and we wonder why it has never before been introduced into horticulture. It is found on the Nueces river in Southwest Texas, where it grows from six to eight feet high. On the lower Rio Grande it grows still higher, and in Mexico it reaches still greater size. Price, $1.

Cape Jasmine—Broad leaved evergreen shrub; bears a large double white flower; very fragrant; a fine yard plant; hardy in Southern Texas; blooms all summer. 50 cents to $1.

Euonymus Japonica—A bright evergreen shrub, with bright green oval leaves. It will grow 8 to 10 feet if allowed to do so, but looks better if kept to a smaller size by occasionally clipping. 25 to 50 cents.

California Privet—Our choice from among all the privets. It makes a beautiful border for a walk or carriage drive, bears any amount of shearing at any time of year. If allowed to grow tall it will reach 6 to 8 feet and makes a good screen. When unsheared it bears, in the Spring, numerous spikes of pure white flowers. 25 cents each; $6.00 per hundred. Large quantities and special sizes at special rates.

Budlyua Lindbyana—An evergreen shrub with long narrow pointed leaves of bright green. It begins early in the Spring to send up numerous small spikes of lilac colored flowers and continues to bloom till the frosts of the following Fall. 50 cents.

Magnolia Grandiflora—The Magnolia of the South; a very fine broad-leaf; leaves large; flowers very large and showy. *It will fail wherever there is too much lime.* We have it doing well on deep sandy soil with clay sub-soil; bloomed with us five years after planting. $1 for pot-raised trees.

Pittosporum—Low, broad-leaved evergreen; is suited to be trained into almost any shape required. For pot-raised plants, $1.

GRASSES.

Gynerium Argenteum (*Pampas Grass*)—A most ornamental plant, with silvery, plume-like spikes of flowers; hardy and thrives in any soil of ordinary fertility. 25 to 50 cents.

Gynerium Roseum (*Rose-colored*)—Flowers of a light rose color. Plumes large and silky. When just appearing they are of a purple tint; this gradually fades until a soft rose tint is attained. 25 to 50 cents.

Erianthus Ravennæ attains a height of ten or twelve feet, throwing up numerous flower spikes of grayish white; flowers profusely and remains a long time; needs space to show its merits. In fact *none* of these grasses should be crowded. 25 to 50 cents.

Eulalia Japonica Zebrina—It forms compact clumps, sometimes six feet in diameter. Its flower stalks are very graceful and numerous. Its leaves are striped and blotched with gold, the stripes running across the leaves. 25 cents.

Lemon Grass—We do not know the proper botanical designation of this grass. We found it on the lower Rio Grande in almost every garden. Over a large extent of country it is steeped and used as *tea*. I was told at Brownsville, Texas, that in large districts of Mexico the Lemon Grass supplied the only tea known to the poor people of that country. The odor and taste of the bruised leaves remind one of orange peel. It is the favorite drink of the writer whose recovery from a long period of debility has been simultaneous with the use of Lemon Grass teas. Perhaps the grass had nothing to do with the improvement, but the writer is firm in the belief that it *has*. A strong succulent stem developing long, broad leaves. A single plant soon develops a large clump, two or three of which are sufficient to supply a large family with tea. I have never been able to learn of its having flowered in Mexico or Texas. It is propagated by division. 25 cents.

ROSES

The climate of Texas is well suited to the rose. The annual bloomers so valued at the North are not generally desirable here, not because they fail but because we have such a wealth of constant bloomers that are no more trouble to care for and reward our efforts with so much greater liberality.

Sandy loam is the best soil for roses, and yet they will flourish in almost any soil with proper preparation and care. Old, well-rotted, barnyard manure is excellent; but never apply fresh animal manure to your rose plants. Old, well rotted, chip manure, such as will be found about many old kitchen wood piles is good.

When to plant. In our climate the question of fall or spring planting has little or no force. The main point is to let the vegetation become thoroughly checked by frost before removing the plants. Many customers go wild about getting their plants "*early.*" They insist upon the nurseryman delivering *early*, and then afterwards complain because they have lost their plants.

Again, some wait till the Spring growth has begun when it is hazardous to subject the plants to the exposure incident to removal. Avoid both of these extremes. Every nurseryman should have knowledge enough upon the subject to know when his plants are *ready* for removal, and should value his reputation sufficiently to *insist* upon his rights in this particular. But do not urge him into delivering the plants in an immature state, and then blame him for your own fault in the matter.

Planting should be carefully done. Don't let the roots be exposed to the sun or wind. Plants received in good order are often lost between the interval of unpacking and final planting.

If you are in doubt how to plant them please consult our chapter entitled *How to Plant a Tree.*

Cultivate Well. Whoever intends the best success must not only give his roses rich soil, but must cultivate the soil thoroughly or expect only partial success. We cultivate our roses with plow cultivator and hoe several times every season—in fact, as often as conditions seem to require, keeping the soil loose in the immediate region of the plants, and free from weeds and grass. Where the plow and cultivator cannot go we let the grubbing hoe or spading fork do the work.

Pruning is important at planting time. We usually cut our plant sufficiently before they leave our hands. But if we fail to do so the planter should so cut them that they have not more than three or four shoots remaining, at most, and *two* canes are still better. And even these should be shortened to not more than two or three eyes each.

The above remarks apply to the time of planting solely; but also every year there should be a careful pruning. The best season for pruning here is from the middle or last of December to the first of February. It may be done at any time before the Spring growth begins.

Climbing and Pillar Roses need comparatively little pruning, and yet that little should not be neglected. It is not often that we would shorten in a healthy climber, except at the end of the leading shoots when they seem disposed to run farther than is desired, or the side shoots to prevent too much extension in a given direction, or to prevent a more crowded foliage than may be desire. Sometimes it is best to remove more or less side shoots altogether if the plant seems weakening. When it is desired that a removed side shoot should, in course, be restored, then its removal should be so made as to retain two or more eyes. When it is desired to have a more dense growth of foliage then all the shoots may be cut back more or less to induce sub laterals. In cutting back always cut just above a bud and avoid leaving sharp points. When a sharp point has been unintentionally made it can be remedied by a second cut.

Hybrid Remontant Roses require different treatment. If the *very earliest* blooming is required in the Spring some of the canes of the former year's growth should be retained quite or altogether entire, while the greater number should be cut back to within two eyes of the old wood.

If *abundant blooming* is required without regard to the size of the flowers, the weak shoots only should be cut out and the strong canes cut back about a fourth of the last year's growth. (Remember that this work is supposed to be done *in winter.*) By the above treatment the flowers will be small but very abundant and showy.

But if the flowers are required to be as large and perfect as possible, the weak wood should all be removed, and all of the strong ones of last year's growth cut back to within two or three eyes of the old wood.

China Roses, and all having a bushy habit, we manage upon another plan. If a large bush is required we let it grow up at will, thinning out the tops only when they become too crowded, and remove any dead or dying wood. Some varieties will, in this way, attain an enormous size. We have a Louis Phillippe that sometimes has about 1,000 roses at once. But most persons do not want their roses to attain such proportions.

If it is required to confine them to a limited space then I would follow the plan of cutting out the oldest wood and preserving the new whenever a reduction of the size of the bush was desired, of course waiting for the proper conditions of growth under which to do the work.

The Bourbon Roses are impatient of much cutting, and therefore we confine our cutting mostly to the removal of dead or dying portions.

Removing Rose Buds. Some imagine that it will injure their plants to let them bloom heavily, and they therefore remove the young rose buds to prevent blooming, in order to strengthen the plant. To such we will say that it does the plants no harm to bloom. But when a bloom is fully matured and begins to drop its petal, this is the signal that the plant has begun to *form seed*, and the formation of *seeds does* tax the energy of the plant. Therefore remove this dilapidated rose at once, and remove every *seed bud* that you discover, so as to preserve every energy of the plant for the production of flowers.

OUR ROSES.

We have cultivated a large number of varieties on our premises, and found so many of them so much resembling each other that we have concentrated our efforts at propagation upon a smaller number that are more clearly distinct.

In every department of horticulture there are always some *specialists* whose great "*specialty*" seems to be to laud the praises of some NEW variety which they offer at rare rates. Next, when their bubble bursts, they select another and then another. Sometimes they take up some old variety, giving it a new name if the purpose requires it, and having just discovered that it has very special merits, they sing its virtues for a season—and so they go on from year to year wringing money from a too credulous public.

The rose trade is not exempt from such adventurers. We have made investments in these articles of short-lived glory that have cost us their weight in gold. And yet none of the solid improvements that we have ever made in building up our collections in any department have come from these *noisy* specialists.

We *originate* no roses. We obtain our original stock from those who do sufficient business to afford to keep a corps of professional rose growers who are competent to test the material passing through their hands, and who make up their lists under every advantage. Having secured varieties that bear the tests of *our* region, we then add them to our list for propagation for our trade.

We disseminate no cheap, hot-house, *baby* rose plants, but supply with *open ground field plants* that will give satisfaction whenever our customers give them the proper conditions of success.

LISTS OF ROSES.

Prices of Roses.—At nursery, strong plants, 50 cents each; $5 per dozen except where otherwise stated. Rare varieties not named in this list and special assortments will be supplied at special rates.

CHINA, TEA, AND BOURBON ROSES..

Aristides—White, buff center; Tea.

Azelia Imbert—Canary yellow; Tea.

Cheshunt Hybrid—Cherry carmine, shaded violet; of vigorous growth, very large rose, free Spring bloomer, but rarely blooms in Summer. Hybrid Tea.

Capt. Christie—Flesh, with deeper center; free bloomer, fine flower, dwarf, thornless. Hybrid Tea. $1.00.

Climbing Devoniensis—See Noisette and other Perpetual Climbers.

Duchere—White, free bloomer. China.

Empress Eugenie—Large, very full, beautifully cupped; delicate rose; an extra good flowerer. Bourbon.

Etoile de Lyon—Large, full, canary yellow. Tea.

Louis Phillippe—Dark crimson, often silvered center. China.

Madame Alfred Corrier—Pure white, sometimes tinged with flesh; very free and constant bloomer. Hybrid Tea.

Marshal Niel—Deep canary yellow, sometimes a tinge of pink shading; large and full, a free bloomer, has not generally succeeded with us on its own roots. We supply it only budded on strong stocks. Climbing Tea. 75 cents each.

Pink Daily—Pretty buds; not a fine rose but desirable on account of its extra blooming habits. China.

Picayune—Pale pink; very small, often not larger than a dime; double; a cute little curiosity; constant bloomer. China.

Perle de Lyon—Dark yellow; one of our best yellow Teas.

Zelia Pradel—One of our purest white roses; half climber. Tea. When ordered alone 75 cents.

HYBRID REMONTANT ROSES.

This class should comprise the main bulk of every collection. They are all hardy, upright growers and produce large flowers.

Achille Gonod—Lilac rose; very large bloom; good bloomer; one of the best.

August Von Gert—Bright lilac rose.

Adam Paul—Large, open flower, pink, good bloomer.

Blach de Meru—Light flesh.

Belle of Normandy—Lilac pink, large and sweet.

Bessie Johnson—Light blush.

Crown Prince—Purplish crimson.

Duc de Cazes—Purplish red, shaded violet; dwarf growth.

Dr. Sewell—Crimson scarlet, shade purple.

Duke of Connaught—Deep crimson, velvety; dwarf habit; not a very free bloomer.

Fanny Pitzold—Clear satin rose.

Gen. Jacqueminot—Fiery red; an old popular variety much called for, but we think there are several better roses.

Infant of Mt. Carmel—Clear, bright rosy pink; large and very double; an old rose but too good to lay aside.

John Nesmith—Brilliant deep red.

Louis Odier—Clear satin rose.

La Reine—Deep rosy lilac; a standard old variety.

Marshal Suchet—Deep carmine pink.

Magna Charta—Bright pink.

Madame Moreau—Deep brilliant carmine, changes to purple; perpetual bloomer; our favorite of its class. 75 cents.

Princess Louise Victoria—Deep crimson changing lighter.

Princess Mathilde—Dark crimson shaded purple.

Prince Albert—Deep crimson.

Paul Neyron—Deep pink; one of our very largest roses.

Perle des Blanches—Pure white; free bloomer; a strong competitor of Zelia Pradel.

Peonia—Crimson red.

Prince Camille de Rohan—One of our darkest crimson roses.

Sidonie—Light pink; our favorite of its color and class.

Vulcan—Velvety crimson changing to purple.

NOISETTE AND OTHER PERPETUAL CLIMBERS.

Chromatella or Cloth of Gold—Very large; chrome yellow; budded on manetti. 75 cents.

Climbing Devoniensis—Tea, white, creamy center.

James Sprunt—A climbing China, dark crimson.

Jules Jurgensen—Magenta-centered shaded violet.

Marechal Niel—Deep canary yellow; large and full; a free bloomer; grows best budded on some strong stock.

Octavia—Deep crimson, strong grower; small double flower; very constant bloomer.

Reine Marie Henriette—Bright cherry red, good form and vigorous habit.

Woodland Margaret—White, vigorous; a very constant bloomer.

POLYANTHA ROSES.

A new class of roses produced by crossing the Japan type and Texas.

Cecile Brunner—Flowers about one and a half inches in diameter; salmon pink, deeper center; beautifully formed.

Mignonette—Delicate rose changing to blush; flowers very small, blooming enormous profusion. Almost constantly in bloom during the whole growing season.

Paquerette—Pure white; flowers very small; free bloomer.

ANNUAL BLOOMING ROSES.

Valuable at the North but should never be planted here where we have such a wealth of free bloomers. We carry only a very small stock of these roses, confining ourselves altogether to such as are most called for. We feel that every customer who buys one is getting nothing for his money. We put them into our list only because the demand requires it. We shall be glad when the demand ceases altogether.

George the Fourth—Dark velvety crimson, changes to purple; a beautiful flower; blooms splendidly for about two weeks and then waits for the following year.

Mrs. Hovey—Medium size flower; variegated carmine; a very strong grower; we use it as a stock on which to bud Marshal Niel.

Queen of the Prairie—Clear bright pink, large, compact, very double and full; blooms in clusters; is one of the finest of all the Prairie roses.

Seven Sisters—Small flowers in large clusters; varies in color from white to crimson.

MOSS ROSES

For several years we maintained a quite full collection of Moss Roses. We have not been pleased with their general behavior. Most of them are Spring bloomers, but a few of them bloom occasionally and are *called* Perpetual.

Eugene de Savoie—Pink.

Salet—Pale rose, perpetual.

Glory of Mosses—Light pink, compact habit.

Zobride—Pink.

ENTRANCE VIEW TO THE MISSION VALLEY NURSERIES.

INDEX

98; Dowling's June, 98; Elma,
98; Galveston, 25, 98; Gilbert,
25; Guadalupe, 98; La
Magnifique, 98; La Reine, 99;
Lilard's October, 98; Lula, 98;
Maggie Burt, 99; Onderdonk's
Favorite, 25, 99; Orman, 99;
Rose, 99; Rupley's Cling, 99;
Sander's Cling, 99; Taber's
No. 5, 100; Taber's No. 13,
99; Texas, 25, 99; Victoria,
100
pears, 25, 112-114; *varieties:*
Andrews, 114; Bartlett, 114;
Belle Lucrative, 114; Beurre
Bost, 114; Duchesse
c'Angouleme, 114; Kieffer,
114; Le Conte, 114
peas, 12, 14
pecan trees, in Mexico, 49
pecans, 54
peons, in Mexico, 46
pepper, in Mexico, 30
persimmons, 54; Japan, 130
pineapple trees, in Mexico, 43
planting trees. See trees, when to
plant
plums, 12, 25, 104-108;
varieties: American Plums,
African, 25, 105; Beaty, 107;
Caddo Chief, 106; Chickasaw,
26, 105; Clara, 107; Coletta,
25, 106; Early Red, 25, 106;
Golden Beauty, 25, 107;
Hope, 25; Indian Chief, 107;
Jennie Lucas, 106; Kanawha,
107; Mariana, 106; Munson,
25, 106; Newman, 107; Piram,
106; Saffold, 106; Wild Goose,
106; *Oriental Plums,* 107-108;
Botankie, 108; Kelsey, 108;
Ogan—Botan—Chalot—
Mason—Long-fruited, 108;
Prunus Pissardii, 108; Prunus
Simonii, 109; Virgata, 108

polar limit of perfect development, 77, 78
pomegranates, 130
pomology, 25
Popocatépetl, 50
Port Lavaca, Texas, 8
postmaster, 25
potatoes, 12
potatoes, Irish, 3
prairie hens, 14
Protestant church, 52
pruning peach, plum, apple trees,
66-70
Puenta de Dios, the Bridge of
God, 41
Puryear, Pamela, 26
pyramids, in Mexico, 50

quail, 18
quail, in Mexico, 43
quinces, 115

raccoons, long tailed, 43
Rancho Pajarito, 14
Rascon Mountain, 39
raspberries, 127
reboza, 46
Reconstruction Period, 23
red pepper trees, 35, 51
remuda, 21
reproduction of varieties of fruit
from seed, 87-90
rice, 12
Richmond, Virginia, 3
Roosevelt, Theodore, Jr., 1
roses, 10, 55, 142-150; *varieties:*
Annual Blooming Roses:
George the Fourth, 149; Mrs.
Hovey, 149; Queen of the
Prairie, 149; Seven Sisters,
149; *China, Tea, and Bourbon
Roses:* Aristides, 146, Azelia
Imbert, 146; Capt. Christie,
146; Cheshunt Hybrid, 146;
Climbing Devoniensis, 146;
Duchere, 146; Empress